THE ENCYCLOPEDIA OF PSYCHOACTIVE DRUGS

SERIES 1

The Addictive Personality
Alcohol and Alcoholism
Alcohol Customs and Rituals
Alcohol Teenage Drinking
Amphetamines Danger in the Fast Lane
Barbiturates Sleeping Potion or Intoxicant?
Caffeine The Most Popular Stimulant
Cocaine A New Epidemic
Escape from Anxiety and Stress
Flowering Plants Magic in Bloom
Getting Help Treatments for Drug Abuse
Heroin The Street Narcotic
Inhalants The Toxic Fumes

LSD Visions or Nightmares?
Marijuana Its Effects on Mind & Body
Methadone Treatment for Addiction
Mushrooms Psychedelic Fungi
Nicotine An Old-Fashioned Addiction
Over-The-Counter Drugs Harmless or Hazardous?
PCP The Dangerous Angel
Prescription Narcotics The Addictive Painkillers
Quaaludes The Quest for Oblivion
Teenage Depression and Drugs
Treating Mental Illness
Valium and Other Tranquilizers

SERIES 2

Bad Trips
Brain Function
Case Histories
Celebrity Drug Use
Designer Drugs
The Downside of Drugs
Drinking, Driving, and Drugs
Drugs and Civilization
Drugs and Crime
Drugs and Diet
Drugs and Disease
Drugs and Emotion
Drugs and Pain
Drugs and Perception
Drugs and Pregnancy
Drugs and Sexual Behavior

Drugs and Sleep
Drugs and Sports
Drugs and the Arts
Drugs and the Brain
Drugs and the Family
Drugs and the Law
Drugs and Women
Drugs of the Future
Drugs Through the Ages
Drug Use Around the World
Legalization: A Debate
Mental Disturbances
Nutrition and the Brain
The Origins and Sources of Drugs
Substance Abuse: Prevention and Treatment
Who Uses Drugs?

DRUGS
& THE LAW

GENERAL EDITOR

Professor Solomon H. Snyder, M.D.

*Distinguished Service Professor of
Neuroscience, Pharmacology, and Psychiatry at
The Johns Hopkins University School of Medicine*

•

ASSOCIATE EDITOR

Professor Barry L. Jacobs, Ph.D.

*Program in Neuroscience, Department of Psychology,
Princeton University*

•

SENIOR EDITORIAL CONSULTANT

Joann Rodgers

*Deputy Director, Office of Public Affairs at
The Johns Hopkins Medical Institutions*

THE ENCYCLOPEDIA OF PSYCHOACTIVE DRUGS
SERIES 2

DRUGS
&
THE LAW

NEIL A. GRAUER

CHELSEA HOUSE PUBLISHERS
NEW YORK • NEW HAVEN • PHILADELPHIA

Tennessee Tech. Library
Cookeville, Tenn.

377557

Chelsea House Publishers
EDITOR-IN-CHIEF: Nancy Toff
EXECUTIVE EDITOR: Remmel T. Nunn
MANAGING EDITOR: Karyn Gullen Browne
COPY CHIEF: Juliann Barbato
PICTURE EDITOR: Adrian G. Allen
ART DIRECTOR: Giannella Garrett
MANUFACTURING MANAGER: Gerald Levine

The Encyclopedia of Psychoactive Drugs
SENIOR EDITOR: Jane Larkin Crain

Staff for DRUGS AND THE LAW
ASSOCIATE EDITOR: Paula Edelson
ASSISTANT EDITOR: Laura-Ann Dolce
COPY EDITOR: James Guiry
DEPUTY COPY CHIEF: Ellen Scordato
EDITORIAL ASSISTANT: Susan DeRosa
ASSOCIATE PICTURE EDITOR: Juliette Dickstein
PICTURE RESEARCHER: Toby Chiu
DESIGNER: Victoria Tomaselli
PRODUCTION COORDINATOR: Joseph Romano
COVER ILLUSTRATION: Amanda Wilson

Copyright © 1988 by Chelsea House Publishers, a division of Main Line Book Co.
All rights reserved. Printed and bound in the United States of America.

First Printing

1 3 5 7 9 8 6 4 2

Library of Congress Cataloging in Publication Data

Grauer, Neil A.
  Drugs and the Law.

  (The Encyclopedia of psychoactive drugs. Series 2)
  Bibliography: p.
  Includes index.
  Summary: Discusses past problems and new procedures relating to the legal
control of drug abuse.
  1. Narcotic laws—Juvenile literature. 2. Drugs—
Law and legislation—Juvenile literature. 3. Drug
abuse—Juvenile literature. [1. Drugs—Law and
legislation.   2. Narcotic laws.   3. Drug
abuse] I. Title. II. Series.
K3641.G73   1988   344'.0545   87-38230

ISBN 1-55546-230-8   342.4545

CONTENTS

The designated smoking area of the Chicago Sun Times. Although hundreds of thousands of Americans continue to smoke, most people believe that smoking should now be restricted in the workplace.

FOREWORD

In the Mainstream
of American Life

One of the legacies of the social upheaval of the 1960s is that psychoactive drugs have become part of the mainstream of American life. Schools, homes, and communities cannot be "drug proofed." There is a demand for drugs — and the supply is plentiful. Social norms have changed and drugs are not only available—they are everywhere.

But where efforts to curtail the supply of drugs and outlaw their use have had tragically limited effects on demand, it may be that education has begun to stem the rising tide of drug abuse among young people and adults alike.

Over the past 25 years, as drugs have become an increasingly routine facet of contemporary life, a great many teenagers have adopted the notion that drug taking was somehow a right or a privilege or a necessity. They have done so, however, without understanding the consequences of drug use during the crucial years of adolescence.

The teenage years are few in the total life cycle, but critical in the maturation process. During these years adolescents face the difficult tasks of discovering their identity, clarifying their sexual roles, asserting their independence, learning to cope with authority, and searching for goals that will give their lives meaning.

Drugs rob adolescents of precious time, stamina, and health. They interrupt critical learning processes, sometimes forever. Teenagers who use drugs are likely to withdraw increasingly into themselves, to "cop out" at just the time when they most need to reach out and experience the world.

Protestors smoke marijuana cigarettes at a 1984 "taste-in" in San Francisco. The protest, reflecting the changing opinion of many people, called for the legalization of marijuana.

Fortunately, as a recent Gallup poll shows, young people are beginning to realize this, too. They themselves label drugs their most important problem. In the last few years, moreover, the climate of tolerance and ignorance surrounding drugs has been changing.

Adolescents as well as adults are becoming aware of mounting evidence that every race, ethnic group, and class is vulnerable to drug dependency.

Recent publicity about the cost and failure of drug rehabilitation efforts; dangerous drug use among pilots, air traffic controllers, star athletes, and Hollywood celebrities; and drug-related accidents, suicides, and violent crime have focused the public's attention on the need to wage an all-out war on drug abuse before it seriously undermines the fabric of society itself.

The anti-drug message is getting stronger and there is evidence that the message is beginning to get through to adults and teenagers alike.

The Encyclopedia of Psychoactive Drugs hopes to play a part in the national campaign now under way to educate young people about drugs. Series 1 provides clear and comprehensive discussions of common psychoactive substances, outlines their psychological and physiological effects on the mind and body, explains how they "hook" the user, and separates fact from myth in the complex issue of drug abuse.

Whereas Series 1 focuses on specific drugs, such as nicotine or cocaine, Series 2 confronts a broad range of both social and physiological phenomena. Each volume addresses the ramifications of drug use and abuse on some aspect of human experience: social, familial, cultural, historical, and physical. Separate volumes explore questions about the effects of drugs on brain chemistry and unborn children; the use and abuse of painkillers; the relationship between drugs and sexual behavior, sports, and the arts; drugs and disease; the role of drugs in history; and the sophisticated drugs now being developed in the laboratory that will profoundly change the future.

Each book in the series is fully illustrated and is tailored to the needs and interests of young readers. The more adolescents know about drugs and their role in society, the less likely they are to misuse them.

Joann Rodgers
Senior Editorial Consultant

A page from a medieval manuscript depicting a grape harvest. Even though it is the most widely abused drug ever developed, alcohol has always been a valuable economic commodity.

INTRODUCTION

The Gift of Wizardry
Use and Abuse

JACK H. MENDELSON, M.D.
NANCY K. MELLO, Ph.D.
Alcohol and Drug Abuse Research Center
Harvard Medical School—McLean Hospital

Dorothy to the Wizard:

"I think you are a very bad man," said Dorothy.
"Oh no, my dear; I'm really a very good man; but I'm a very bad Wizard."
—from THE WIZARD OF OZ

Man is endowed with the gift of wizardry, a talent for discovery and invention. The discovery and invention of substances that change the way we feel and behave are among man's special accomplishments, and, like so many other products of our wizardry, these substances have the capacity to harm as well as to help. Psychoactive drugs can cause profound changes in the chemistry of the brain and other vital organs, and although their legitimate use can relieve pain and cure disease, their abuse leads in a tragic number of cases to destruction.

Consider alcohol — available to all and yet regarded with intense ambivalence from biblical times to the present day. The use of alcoholic beverages dates back to our earliest ancestors. Alcohol use and misuse became associated with the worship of gods and demons. One of the most powerful Greek gods was Dionysus, lord of fruitfulness and god of wine. The Romans adopted Dionysus but changed his name to Bacchus. Festivals and holidays associated with Bacchus celebrated the harvest and the origins of life. Time has blurred the images of the Bacchanalian festival, but the theme of drunkenness as a major part of celebration has survived the pagan gods and remains a familiar part of modern society. The term "Bacchanalian Festival" conveys a more appealing image than "drunken orgy" or "pot party," but whatever the label, drinking alcohol is a form of drug use that results in addiction for millions.

The fact that many millions of other people can use alcohol in moderation does not mitigate the toll this drug takes on society as a whole. According to reliable estimates, one out of every ten Americans develops a serious alcohol-related problem sometime in his or her lifetime. In addition, automobile accidents caused by drunken drivers claim the lives of tens of thousands every year. Many of the victims are gifted young people, just starting out in adult life. Hospital emergency rooms abound with patients seeking help for alcohol-related injuries.

Who is to blame? Can we blame the many manufacturers who produce such an amazing variety of alcoholic beverages? Should we blame the educators who fail to explain the perils of intoxication, or so exaggerate the dangers of drinking that no one could possibly believe them? Are friends to blame — those peers who urge others to "drink more and faster," or the macho types who stress the importance of being able to "hold your liquor"? Casting blame, however, is hardly constructive, and pointing the finger is a fruitless way to deal with the problem. Alcoholism and drug abuse have few culprits but many victims. Accountability begins with each of us, every time we choose to use or misuse an intoxicating substance.

It is ironic that some of man's earliest medicines, derived from natural plant products, are used today to poison and to intoxicate. Relief from pain and suffering is one of society's many continuing goals. Over 3,000 years ago, the Therapeutic Papyrus of Thebes, one of our earliest written records, gave instructions for the use of opium in the treatment of pain. Opium, in the form of its major derivative, morphine, and similar compounds, such as heroin, have also been used by many to induce changes in mood and feeling. Another example of man's misuse of a natural substance is the coca leaf, which for centuries was used by the Indians of Peru to reduce fatigue and hunger. Its modern derivative, cocaine, has important medical use as a local anesthetic. Unfortunately, its increasing abuse in the 1980s clearly has reached epidemic proportions.

The purpose of this series is to explore in depth the psychological and behavioral effects that psychoactive drugs have on the individual, and also, to investigate the ways in which drug use influences the legal, economic, cultural, and even moral aspects of societies. The information presented here (and in other books in this series) is based on many clinical and laboratory studies and other observations by people from diverse walks of life.

Over the centuries, novelists, poets, and dramatists have provided us with many insights into the sometimes seductive but ultimately problematic aspects of alcohol and drug use. Physicians, lawyers, biologists, psychologists, and social scientists have contributed to a better understanding of the causes and consequences of using these substances. The authors in this series have attempted to gather and condense all the latest information about drug use and abuse. They have also described the sometimes wide gaps in our knowledge and have suggested some new ways to answer many difficult questions.

One such question, for example, is how do alcohol and drug problems get started? And what is the best way to treat them when they do? Not too many years ago, alcoholics and drug abusers were regarded as evil, immoral, or both. It is now recognized that these persons suffer from very complicated diseases involving deep psychological and social problems. To understand how the disease begins and progresses, it is necessary to understand the nature of the substance, the behavior of addicts, and the characteristics of the society or culture in which they live.

Although many of the social environments we live in are very similar, some of the most subtle differences can strongly influence our thinking and behavior. Where we live, go to school and work, whom we discuss things with — all influence our opinions about drug use and misuse. Yet we also share certain commonly accepted beliefs that outweigh any differences in our attitudes. The authors in this series have tried to identify and discuss the central, most crucial issues concerning drug use and misuse.

Despite the increasing sophistication of the chemical substances we create in the laboratory, we have a long way to go in our efforts to make these powerful drugs work for us rather than against us.

The volumes in this series address a wide range of timely questions. What influence has drug use had on the arts? Why do so many of today's celebrities and star athletes use drugs, and what is being done to solve this problem? What is the relationship between drugs and crime? What is the physiological basis for the power drugs can hold over us? These are but a few of the issues explored in this far-ranging series.

Educating people about the dangers of drugs can go a long way toward minimizing the desperate consequences of substance abuse for individuals and society as a whole. Luckily, human beings have the resources to solve even the most serious problems that beset them, once they make the commitment to do so. As one keen and sensitive observer, Dr. Lewis Thomas, has said,

> There is nothing at all absurd about the human condition. We matter. It seems to me a good guess, hazarded by a good many people who have thought about it, that we may be engaged in the formation of something like a mind for the life of this planet. If this is so, we are still at the most primitive stage, still fumbling with language and thinking, but infinitely capacitated for the future. Looked at this way, it is remarkable that we've come as far as we have in so short a period, really no time at all as geologists measure time. We are the newest, youngest, and the brightest thing around.

DRUGS
&
THE LAW

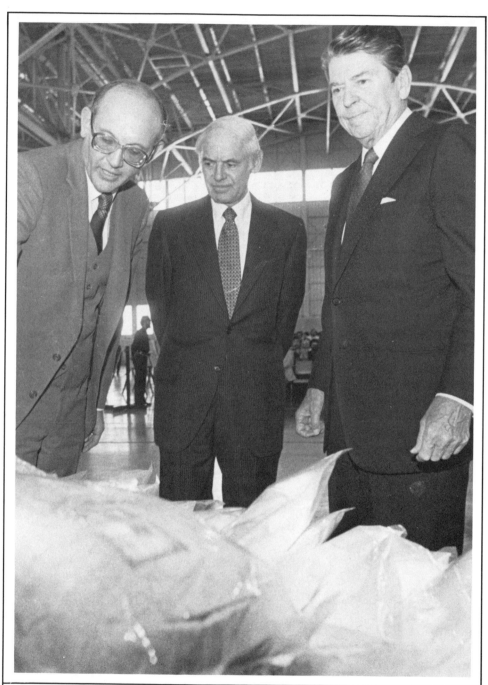

President Ronald Reagan (right), U.S. Attorney General William French Smith (center), and a South Florida Task Force official inspect a cache of confiscated cocaine in an airplane hangar in south Florida.

AUTHOR'S PREFACE

It is a familiar American expression, one that seems to spring automatically from our lips whenever we are angry, frustrated, or appalled about something: "There oughta be a law. . . ."

We are a nation devoted to the law; in love with it, really. As Alexis de Tocqueville, the French aristocrat who toured this country in 1831 and 1832, observed: "There is hardly a . . . question in the United States which does not sooner or later turn into a judicial one." That is still the case. Almost every issue of contemporary society ends up in the courts. We have laws by the thousands — local, state, and federal — and we spend billions of dollars each year to enforce them —or evade them.

The United States is not the only country that does this, of course. Every nation has its own legal system — in many cases ones that are vastly different from ours — and the amount of money spent on law enforcement worldwide is staggering.

Probably the costliest item on the monumental international legal bill is the effort to eliminate illegal drug use. The Pacific Research Institute for Public Policy in San Fran-

Peasants harvest coca leaves in a hillside field in Peru. The use of coca leaves in Peru dates back to the ancient Inca empire, when coca leaves were chewed by workers to ease their hunger and exhaustion.

cisco estimates that the United States alone spends approximately $5.5 billion each year to wage what it and other nations consider a "war" against illegal substance abuse.

The result of this ongoing battle against drugs is at best a stand-off. It is estimated that the trade in illegal drugs — primarily heroin, cocaine, and marijuana in all their various forms — is a $110 billion-a-year business just in the United States. Indeed, despite antidrug laws, the cultivation and sale of the plants that can be processed to make illegal substances are among the biggest businesses in some countries, and even in parts of the United States. For example, coffee may be the "official" top export of Colombia, but in fact cocaine is that nation's biggest source of foreign income — accounting for some 36% of its gross national product, or approximately

$25 billion. Similarly, the illegal marijuana crop in California is worth more than $2 billion, which is more than the value of the annual production of grapes there, supposedly the state's chief agricultural crop.

Age-old Efforts to Control Substance Abuse

Nevertheless, the economic significance of various mind-and-mood altering substances has not prevented governments from trying to outlaw or at least control their use. Some drugs that once were used freely have been banned; others that once were banned are now freely available. Drugs that are permitted in some countries are outlawed in others. Virtually every nation on the globe, however, has laws on drugs — and

SEVERAL

Laws and Orders

Made at the first Sessions of the

GENERAL COURT

Held at *Boston, May* 28. 1679, and published by their Order.

Edward Rawson Secretary.

A page from an antidrinking law passed in colonial Massachussetts in 1679. The lawmakers cited drunkenness as "an abusive and evil practice."

WHereas there is an abusive and evil practice taken up in several places of this Colony, upon Training dayes, more publick or private, & other publick Conventions of People upon civil occasions, diverse persons taking liberty to bring into the field, and other places near such concourse of people, considerable quantityes of wine, strong liquor, Cider, and other inebriating Drinks, having no licence so to doe, whereby many People both English and Indians that come to such Meetings, as well as Souldiers, commit many disorders of Drunkenness, Fighting, neglect of duty, &c. for prevention whereof,

It is Ordered by this Court and the Authority thereof, that henceforth no Person whatsoever shall presume to bring into the field, and sell by re ail upon such occasions, any Wine strong Liquor, Cider or any other inebriating Drink (excepting Beer of a peny a quart) unless he or they so doing have licence from the hands of two Magistrates, or the chief Military Officer or Officers in the Field, upon penalty of forfeiting all such strong Drink, and paying a Fine of five pounds, one half to the informer, the other half to the County Treasury. And it is further Ordered, that the Constables of the Town where such meeting is, are Ordered and required with a meet company to guard him, shall by Warrant from the chief Officer, seize upon all strong Liquors, Wine, Cider, or other strong Drink, and dispose of the sam. as this Law directs.

always has. Ever since the beginning of recorded history — and no doubt even before then — societies have sought to control the distribution of these substances.

The rulers of the ancient Inca empire, an area corresponding to modern Peru, Bolivia, Ecuador, and parts of Colombia and Chile, restricted the chewing of the coca leaf, the plant from which cocaine is derived. Only royalty, the priesthood, and those whose accomplishments merited a reward that "was prized far above the richest presents of silver or gold" were allowed to have coca leaves. Moreover, Inca noblemen were buried with an ample supply of the leaf. Early in the 16th century, when the Spanish explorers known as the *conquistadores* (conquerors) took over the Inca empire, they also took control of the distribution of coca leaves. They gave generous portions of them to the general population in order to keep them happy and make them work longer and harder with less food (since coca, like modern amphetamines,

A 1921 anti-Prohibition march in New York City. Most Americans opposed Prohibition, believing that it did little to wipe out alcohol abuse and much to spread crime, violence, and official corruption.

suppresses hunger). Even today, some workers' contracts in Bolivia require employers to supply a daily ration of coca leaf, as well as a salary, a habit stemming from the Spaniards' practice of paying wages in coca leaves.

Both alcohol and tobacco have been used as currency. Tobacco was used to buy and sell other goods, and in some colonial courts, defendants convicted in criminal cases sometimes were ordered to pay fines in the form of tobacco. Similarly, in colonial times, American workers often got part of their pay in rum or whiskey and were given special days off "to get drunk," as some work agreements explicitly acknowledged. In some western outposts — then in places such as Ohio — goods often were priced in whiskey, which first was distilled in western Pennsylvania and was the easiest and most lucrative way to market grain. Rum, which is distilled from molasses, was the most popular alcoholic beverage then and served for a time as a major medium of exchange. It was central to the economic growth of New England, where much of it was made.

Alcohol and tobacco remain important commodities in our economy, but they also are drugs that can have extremely bad effects. Together they cause more addiction, disease, and death than heroin, cocaine, and marijuana combined. According to Dr. C. Everett Koop, the surgeon general of the United States, cigarettes alone were responsible for 90% of the 360,000 deaths from heart disease and cancer in the United States in 1983. Alcoholism, which afflicts at least 10 million Americans, can destroy both mind and body. Abuse of this drug is in fact the largest law-enforcement problem in the country; up to 55% of all arrests — including drunk-driving charges—are related in some way to alcohol.

Yet unlike heroin, cocaine, and marijuana, alcohol and tobacco are legal. This somehow seems contradictory, given the admitted problems associated with alcohol and tobacco use, but they remain legal (although greater restrictions now are being placed on their use), probably because of their thoroughly ingrained acceptance as part of our society's culture. Although heroin, cocaine, marijuana, and other now-illegal substances were not unlawful at the beginning of this century, they were never an accepted part of American society.

The Noble Experiment

Another reason alcohol is legal in this country is that our attempt to outlaw alcoholic beverages — the 13 year "noble experiment" of national prohibition — was such a spectacular failure. People simply refused to consider the possession and consumption of a bottle of beer or a pint of whiskey as a criminal act comparable to robbing a bank or burglarizing a home. Not only did Prohibition fail to end alcohol use between 1920 and 1933, but it also encouraged the growth of organized crime, providing the huge profits that helped gangsters branch out into the narcotics business once their trade in illegal liquor dried up with the repeal of the Prohibition laws.

The failure of Prohibition is often cited by those who think it is useless to continue the worldwide war on illegal drugs as it is now being waged. "For thousands of years people have taken substances to improve or heighten their feelings. And they always will, despite attempts to prevent, dissuade or penalize them," wrote Brian Freemantle, an investigative journalist from Great Britain who conducted a thorough probe of the illegal drug trade.

The Debate over Legalization

Nevertheless, many law enforcement officials insist that the only way to combat the world's exploding drug problem is to be even more relentless in the crackdown on the peddlers and users of illegal drugs. To some observers, however, this is a hopeless battle. Although Freemantle and others do not advocate the legalization of all the currently illegal drugs, acknowledging as they do the terrible economic and physical costs of drug addiction, they think something other than the current laws and penalties against drug use should be tried. Perhaps a system allowing doctors to prescribe heroin or cocaine to addicts should be adopted. A system along these lines has been used in Great Britain for heroin addicts — with considerably mixed results, as Chapter 4 will describe. In the case of marijuana, which is viewed by some, correctly or incorrectly, as a relatively harmless drug, perhaps the thing to do would be to decriminalize its use — which is not the same thing as legalization.

In the United States alone, it is estimated that the social, economic, health, and crime-related costs of drug abuse now run to between $10 and $20 billion *each year.* Although those who question the effectiveness of the present law enforcement effort against illegal drugs offer no foolproof solution to these problems, their argument is that whatever the answer to the illegal drug epidemic may be, it is not what we are doing now.

The cover from the Temperance Almanac of 1875. Most temperance societies required their members to make a pledge promising to cut down or stop their consumption of "demon rum."

CHAPTER 1

PROHIBITION — HOW DRY WE WEREN'T

Given the sorry history of Prohibition, one may wonder why laws banning alcoholic beverages were ever passed. Were they the work of some fast-footed, moralizing fanatics who somehow steamrolled an unsuspecting country into outlawing beer, wine, and liquor?

The answer is no. Prohibition, which became the law of the land when the 18th Amendment to the Constitution was ratified in 1919, was the logical result of a well-established, increasingly powerful political movement that spent many years urging moderate use and then total abstinence from alcohol. Beginning first in town and city councils, then moving up to state legislatures, and finally going to the U.S. Congress in Washington, the advocates of alcohol abolition succeeded in persuading the people's representatives that the country wanted to try prohibition — as most of the country then probably did. As the historian Sean Dennis Cashman has written, the medical arguments for prohibition found favor with doctors, scientists, intellectuals, and humanitarians; businessman and factory owners found economic arguments for prohibition persuasive; religious reasons were advanced by evangelists, puritans, and many rural residents; and reformers of every sort were impressed by the social and political arguments in favor of it.

Almost as soon as Prohibition became a reality, however, people tried to evade it — and more often than not they succeeded. They also soon saw that the 18th Amendment did more harm than good. "They had expected to be greeted ... by ... angels bearing gifts of peace, happiness, prosperity and salvation, which they had been assured would be theirs when the rum demon had been scotched," wrote the historian Herbert Asbury. "Instead they were met by a horde of bootleggers, moonshiners, rum-runners, hijackers, gangsters, racketeers, trigger men, venal judges, corrupt police, crooked politicians, and speak-easy operators, all bearing the twin symbols of the 18th Amendment — the Tommy gun and the poisoned cup."

"A Good Creature of God"

When European settlers first arrived in North America, they brought alcoholic beverages with them. The Pilgrims' provisions on the *Mayflower* in 1620 included beer, which children as well as adults drank. Alcohol was an important part of the colonial diet, considered by many to be a cure-all for every ailment and a "good creature of God," as some colonial laws put it. Even the puritanical Pilgrim fathers, who passed laws forbidding many supposedly wicked pleasures, permitted alcohol to go unregulated, except for laws that forbade drunkenness.

That there was not more open drunkenness in colonial times is amazing, because alcohol consumption was part of every social, political, and religious event. Town meetings and even court hearings were frequently held in taverns, and church events featured great quantities of alcoholic beverages. People "seldom went more than a few hours without a drink," according to one historian.

This custom continued in the United States into the early 19th century. One study in 1810 found that more than 33.3 million gallons of hard liquor a year were drunk in the homes of the nation's 7.2 million inhabitants — or some 4.7 gallons per person. Another study, done in 1826, found that the people of Albany, New York, drank 200,000 gallons of alcohol that year — an average of 10 gallons for every man, woman, and child in the city!

A replica of the hatchet used by Carrie Nation. Nation, a prominent antiliquor crusader, was well known for attacking saloons with bricks, iron bars, stones, and, of course, her hatchet.

The Move Toward Temperance

With so much drinking — and surely a great deal of drunkenness — going on, it is not surprising that many people wanted at least to curb the consumption of alcohol. Temperance societies were founded in New York, Connecticut, Massachusetts, Pennsylvania, Rhode Island, Vermont, New Hampshire, and Maine. Each required its members to take a "pledge" in which they promised to cut down or stop their drinking. One group, the American Temperance Society, had a branch in the Michigan territory that changed its original pledge, which permitted moderate drinking, to one that called for total abstinence from alcohol. Its members were listed on the group's roster as either "O.P.," which stood for the old pledge, or "T-Total," or temperance-total, meaning they had vowed to avoid all alcoholic beverages. Soon they became known as "teetotalers," a term that spread and still applies to those who refrain entirely from alcohol. By 1836, the American Temperance Society had more than a million members, many of whom considered drinking a sinful act, and viewed the temperance cause as a religious crusade.

A jacket used during the 1920s to smuggle liquor into the country. For many drinkers, Prohibition was little more than a stumbling block that they easily found ways to avoid.

The first state prohibition law was passed in Maine in 1851. It forbade the manufacture or sale of alcoholic beverages within the state, imposed heavy fines and prison terms for violators, and permitted authorities to confiscate and destroy any illegal liquor they seized. The "Maine law" became a model for other state legislatures, and by 1855 twelve more states had adopted prohibition: New Hampshire, Vermont, Connecticut, New York, Delaware, Indiana, Iowa, Massachusetts, Michigan, Minnesota, Nebraska, and Rhode Island. (A similar law was narrowly defeated in Illinois, where a legislator — and future president — named Abraham Lincoln wrote a prohibition bill that was passed by the legislature but defeated by the citizens in a popular referendum.) Within a few years, however, some of these state prohibition laws were overturned in the courts; other were repealed; still others were made less severe. Only Maine made its prohibition law part of its state constitution and retained its ban on alcohol.

The prohibition movement stalled in the mid-1850s, when issues such as slavery became more important and eventually led to the Civil War. After the war ended in 1865, the temperance movement began to grow again. The Prohibition party (which still nominates candidates in many state and local elections) was founded in 1869; the Women's Christian Temperance Union was founded in 1874; and in 1893, those who sought the abolition of saloons, the often dirty and sometimes violent gathering places where much of the country's liquor was sold, created the Anti-Saloon League, which became the most powerful prohibition organization.

One of the prohibition movement's most colorful figures was Carrie Nation, who was a prominent antiliquor crusader in the early 20th century. She was a Kentuckian who lived in Missouri for many years, but she did much of her crusading in Kansas, where she went saloon-bashing with bricks, iron bars, stones and, eventually, her famous hatchet. Although Kansas had officially banned liquor by constitutional amendment in 1880, it did have scores of illegal speakeasies and saloons in business and these were what Carrie Nation attacked. After smashing bottles, barrels, and glassware in Kansas, she showed up in towns and cities all over the country, brandishing her hatchet and destroying saloons and speakeasies wherever she went, inspiring others to adopt the prohibition cause — if perhaps less violently. She was a nationally — indeed internationally — known figure by the time of her death in 1911.

In 1913, the Anti-Saloon League issued a call for national prohibition. Working within state legislatures as a lobbying group, it succeeded in persuading some 16 states to adopt prohibition laws just before the United States entered World War I in 1917. During the war, patriotic appeals to save grain and remain sober for the war effort added momentum to the national prohibition cause. The goal of the movement was a constitutional amendment that would ban alcoholic beverages nationwide. By 1919, 31 states already had prohibition laws on their books. The prohibitionists, known as "drys," triumphed when Congress adopted the 18th Amendment to the Constitution in December 1917, and 36 states ratified it by January 1919. (Eventually, 46 of the 48 states then in existence ratified the 18th Amendment, with only Rhode Island and Connecticut refusing to do so.)

Curiously, the 18th Amendment did not directly prohibit the possession of alcohol or the drinking of it. Rather, it prohibited the "manufacture, sale, or transportation of intoxicating liquors in the United States" and gave both the federal government and the state governments the power to enforce the legislation. Doctors could prescribe alcohol for medicinal uses, and people who made wine for their own private consumption were still legally allowed to do so.

Doomed to Failure

It was apparent from the outset that Prohibition was doomed to failure. Federal enforcement of Prohibition, which took effect on January 17, 1920, was tainted by indifference and corruption. The day after enforcement policies took effect, the newspapers reported the first seizures of illegal liquor and liquor-making equipment in New York, Illinois, Michigan, and Indiana. Within 10 days, three federal Prohibition agents in Chicago were indicted for accepting bribes and selling confiscated whiskey to illegal liquor merchants known as bootleggers. Three weeks later, two more federal agents were arrested in Baltimore on charges of corruption. In sum, the arrival of Prohibition marked the beginning of what one historian has called "corruption on a scale unparalleled in American history."

"Prohibition's Fairest Flower"

In no city was the corruption of the so-called Roaring Twenties more in evidence than in Chicago, where the decade's "roar" echoed with the blasts from mobsters' machine guns. Rival gangs of criminals at first divided up the city and its surrounding communities into distinct territories, where each organization could operate its illegal liquor and beer trade. For several years this arrangement worked fairly peacefully; the gangsters earned millions of dollars and bought themselves legal protection by bribing law enforcement officials and politicians.

Violence erupted, however, when the gangsters grew greedy and began trying to invade each others' territories. Savage gangland wars went on for more than five years, from 1924 to 1929. Some 500 men were killed, 300 of them in 1926 and 1927 alone.

By far the most famous of the gangsters was Al Capone, "Prohibition's fairest flower," in the words of Herbert Asbury.

A crime commission in Chicago later estimated that Capone made at least $60 million a year from liquor, narcotics, prostitution, and other illegal operations, with some two-thirds of his take coming from alcohol. For a while Capone was something of a folk hero, known for his extravagant attire, flashy automobiles, and enormous expenditures of money. He was also admired for his candor. "I make my money supplying a popular demand," he said. "If I break the law, my customers are as guilty as I am. When I sell liquor, it's bootlegging. When my patrons serve it on silver trays . . . it's called hospitality."

The public's admiration turned to disgust, however, as the gang wars grew more brutal. The bloodiest incident of the struggles occurred on February 14, 1929 — St. Valentine's Day — in a Chicago garage, where men from Capone's mob machine-gunned to death six members of a rival gang and an innocent bystander. After that, Capone's star began to dim swiftly and he became the object of scorn, even though the murders could never be pinned upon him directly. The Chicago Crime Commission branded him "Public Enemy Number One" (the first time that colorful classification was used),

Al Capone, perhaps the best known of the organized crime figures who profited from the sale of illegal liquor during Prohibition. He was the first person to be dubbed "Public Enemy Number One."

and he left Chicago only to find that he was unwelcome almost everywhere he went. In October 1931, federal authorities charged him with failing to pay income taxes on all the illegal money he had earned — a crime he never even considered—and he was found guilty and sent to prison.

Public support for prohibition had never been wholehearted, and the corruption that ensued after the amendment became law served to undermine that support even further. In addition, the poor, even poisonous, quality of the illegally made liquor that many people drank increased the number of deaths due to alcohol. Moreover, the total number of alcoholics was also on the rise. To the general public, Prohibition seemed to compound the nation's alcohol problem, not redress it.

As some historians have noted, however, the statistics about the effects of Prohibition could be interpreted to bolster both the arguments of the "drys," who favored it, and of the "wets," who opposed it. As Herbert Asbury cynically observed, "The drys lied to make prohibition look good; the wets lied to make it look bad; the government officials lied to make themselves look good and to frighten Congress into giving them more money to spend; and the politicians lied through force of habit."

No amount of statistical sleight-of-hand on either side could hide or further emphasize the fact that Prohibition was not working. But although the tide was turning against Prohibition, its doom was not really sealed until the stock market crash of October 1929 and the Great Depression that followed it. Wets argued that repealing the 18th Amendment would create thousands of jobs in the brewing and liquor industries, as well as supply the federal treasury with millions of dollars in alcohol-related taxes. Prohibition dragged on for a few more years, but in 1932 the Democratic party's presidential candidate, Franklin D. Roosevelt, vowed to seek repeal of the 18th Amendment, and his election assured the end of Prohibition. Within nine months of Roosevelt's inauguration in March 1933, the 21st Amendment to the Constitution was ratified, repealing the 18th.

Some states, counties, and towns, however, still retained local prohibition. Mississippi did not repeal statewide prohibition until 1966, and Kansas finally allowed its counties

During his 1932 campaign for the presidency, Democratic candidate Franklin D. Roosevelt promised to end Prohibition if elected to office. Nine months after his inauguration, the 21st Amendment to the Constitution was ratified, repealing the 18th.

to authorize the sale of liquor by the drink in 1987 — 106 years after the Kansas state constitution proclaimed: "The open saloon shall be and is hereby forever prohibited." (For years, bars and restaurants got around that law by pretending they were private clubs and not "open saloons.") Still, 69 of Kansas's 105 counties remain dry, and West Virginia and Utah still ban the sale of liquor by the drink statewide.

Debating the Legal Drinking Age

Once Prohibition was repealed, most states set the legal drinking age at 21, the same age at which people officially became adults and could vote. Following World War II, a movement began to lower the voting age and, simultaneously, the drinking age. The growing opposition to the Vietnam War in the late 1960s and early 1970s, and the explosion of the "youth culture" gave impetus to the movement. The argument was that if a young man was old enough to be drafted into the armed forces and fight in a war, he was old enough to vote in a presidential election. If that were the case, the argument went, those who could fight in a war and vote for president should also be able to buy a drink. When the voting age was lowered to 18 in 1971, many states began lowering the legal drinking age to 18, too.

By the late 1970s, however, an alarming rise in teenage alcoholism and the number of alcohol-related motor vehicle accidents prompted a reconsideration of the legal drinking age. Since 1980, 31 states have raised their minimum legal drinking age to 21. Now 43 states and the District of Columbia have a minimum legal drinking age of 21. Three states — Colorado, Ohio, and South Dakota — specify 21 as the legal drinking age for distilled spirits (hard liquor) but have lower drinking ages for beer. Three states — Idaho, Wyoming, and Montana — have a legal minimum drinking age of 19. Only Louisiana, which set its drinking age at 18 in 1948, has maintained that age.

Unfortunately, teen drinking and driving remains a serious problem in the 1980s, despite the more stringent laws. Studies show, for example, that more than half of all fatal highway crashes involving two or more vehicles are alcohol-

A drunk driver plowed into this window display set up by the group Students Against Drunk Driving (SADD) in California. Each year, 5,000 teenagers are killed and 130,000 injured in drunk driving accidents.

Candy Lightner, founder of Mothers Against Drunk Driving, with Senator Richard Lugar and Secretary of Transportion Elizabeth Dole, advocates raising the national drinking age to 21 at a Capitol press conference.

related. In addition, 1 in 16 high school seniors drinks alcohol every day; 3.3 million teenagers are known to be alcoholics; adolescence is the only age group with an average life expectancy that is shorter than it was 20 years ago; the leading cause of death among 15- to 24-year-olds is drunk driving. According to the National Safety Council, 5,000 teenagers are killed and 130,000 are injured each year in drunken driving accidents. Every 20 minutes, someone dies in an alcohol-related accident, and figures show that teenagers are involved in a larger number of alcohol-related traffic accidents than any other age group.

A group that has been actively involved in the campaign to raise the drinking age is Mothers Against Drunk Driving (MADD), founded in 1980 by Candy Lightner, a woman from Sacramento, California, whose daughter was killed in a traffic accident that was the fault of a chronic drunk driver. MADD, which now has branches in every state, has been a vocal advocate for higher drinking ages and tougher penalties for drunk drivers. It was, in fact, one of many groups that in 1984 successfully persuaded Congress to pass the National Mini-

Many states, including Massachussetts, have raised the drinking age to 21 in order to reduce the number of teenage highway fatalities.

mum Drinking Age Act, which encourages states to raise their drinking age by giving Congress power to deny federal highway funds to states that have not set the minimum drinking age at 21.

Spreading the Responsibility

In addition to laws concerning the minimum drinking age, legislation exists — both in the United States and in some other countries — that makes those who serve alcoholic beverages partly responsible for what an intoxicated person to whom they gave liquor later does. Some of these laws have been in effect in the United States since the 19th century, when local governments passed so-called dram shop laws, which made tavern keepers financially liable to the families of "habitual drunkards" if the bartenders continued to sell liquor to someone they had been told was an alcoholic. One hundred years later, some 38 states either have a "dram shop" or related laws on the books; the purpose of this legislation is to establish the liability of someone who serves liquor to an alcoholic or even supplies enough liquor to a nonalcoholic to make him or her drunk.

In several test cases, these liability laws have been upheld. For example, a California court has held that an employer who served liquor at an office Christmas party had to pay damages to an employee who was involved in a traffic accident on the way home. In Texas, a court found that a company that sent an intoxicated worker home because he was too drunk to do his job was liable for the damages caused by a traffic accident the man had when he left work. In a potentially far-reaching 1984 case, the New Jersey Supreme Court expanded the liability of liquor-servers to include private citizens who "directly serve" alcohol to a guest and then allow that person to drive off in an impaired condition. In a ruling that has since been established in six other states, the New Jersey court held that a host or hostess is liable for injuries to others caused by a traffic accident involving his or her drunken guest.

In July 1985, the American Bar Association (ABA) urged that criminal penalties for serving alcohol or drugs to a minor be increased. The ABA also recommended that states pass laws authorizing judges to revoke or suspend, completely or partially, the driver's license of people under the age of 21 who are convicted of an alcohol- or drug-related traffic offense or who refuse to undergo substance-testing procedures, such as a breath test, under existing state laws. The ABA also urges states that do not have dram shop or host-liability laws to pass legislation that would make liable for damages someone who sells or serves alcoholic beverages to a person whom the server knows or should know is under the legal drinking age, if that person later becomes drunk and injures himself, another person, or another person's property.

Given these developments and the wave of publicity concerning the dangers of alcohol in general, it seems not only likely but probable that the laws against drunk driving, and the penalties imposed on drunk drivers, will get tougher in the future.

Sigmund Freud, the founder of psychoanalysis, tried for 45 years to quit his 20-cigar-a-day habit, but was unable to do so. Consequently, he spent the last 16 years of his life battling mouth cancer.

CHAPTER 2

TOBACCO: SMOKE GETS IN YOUR EYES

Of all the drugs discussed in this book, the most addictive — and perhaps the most deadly — is nicotine, the psychoactive compound in tobacco.

The U.S. Department of Health and Human Services estimates that more than 300,000 Americans a year die prematurely from smoking-related cancer, cardiovascular disease (involving the heart and circulatory system), and chronic lung ailments. Yet millions of us continue to smoke. A former heroin addict (and former smoker) once told the *New York Times* why: "It was much easier to quit heroin than cigarettes." The craving for nicotine is such that cigarette smokers, unlike those addicted to other drugs, are not satisfied with a daily supply of what they need; they must have a smoke almost every waking hour — at least 15 cigarettes a day. No country into which tobacco has been introduced — either in the form of pipe tobacco, cigars, snuff, chewing tobacco, or cigarettes—has ever been able to give it up.

Mark Twain, a cigar smoker, used to joke that he knew it was easy to quit smoking because he had done it so many times. The bittersweet humor in that jest is lost when the smoking history of Dr. Sigmund Freud, the founding father of psychoanalysis, is considered. Freud smoked as many as 20 cigars a day. In 1894, when he was 38, his physician

A 1747 engraving depicting the Indians making a gift of tobacco to Virginia planters. The Indians are credited with introducing both tobacco and the habit of smoking it in a pipe to the early settlers.

warned Freud that he had developed an irregular heart beat because of his smoking and told him to stop. Freud tried to quit but failed. Within seven weeks he was smoking again. On another occasion, Freud quit smoking for more than a year — but then started again, even though he admitted to friends that it not only harmed his heart but interfered with his studies.

In 1923, when he was 67, Freud developed mouth cancer and underwent the first of what would total 33 operations for cancer of the mouth and jaw. Eventually, Freud's entire jaw was removed and replaced with an artificial one; he was in constant pain, and often he could not speak, chew, or swallow. But he continued to smoke what one of his friends called "an endless series of cigars." Freud died of cancer in 1939 at the age of 83. For 45 years he had tried to quit smoking and could not, even when it made the last 16 years of his life miserable.

Spreading Tobacco Use Around the Globe

When Christopher Columbus first arrived in North America, he (and the explorers who followed him) found the native Indians putting smoking rolls of dried leaves between their lips and puffing away on them. Other Indians put the leaves in a pipe and smoked them that way. The explorers got over their initial astonishment, found this practice fascinating, tried it, and liked it. When some Indians were persuaded to visit London in the 16th century, they had to take their tobacco with them. Its use soon became common there and elsewhere in Europe, as sailors brought back huge cargos of tobacco leaves and seeds. As European exploration began to span the globe, so did the use of tobacco, which the sailors took with them everywhere.

Tobacco use also had its opponents from the very beginning. King James I of England despised it and wrote a stinging attack against it entitled *Counterblaste to Tobacco* in 1604. In the quaint spelling of that day, he vigorously (and accurately) denounced tobacco use as a "custome Lothsome to the eye, hatefull to the Nose, harmefull to the braine, dangerous to the Lungs, and in the blacke stinking fume thereof, neerest resembling the horrible [hellish] smoke of the pit that is bottomelesse."

King James did not try to ban tobacco but other rulers did — and the laws against tobacco proved no more successful than the ones against alcohol. In 1642, Pope Urban VIII issued

King James I of England was scathing in his attack on tobacco use, published in the 1604 treatise Counterblaste to Tobacco.

a formal proclamation against tobacco, and Pope Innocent X issued another one in 1650 — to no great effect. (In 1725, Pope Benedict XIII, who liked to take snuff, voided all the earlier edicts against tobacco.) Some European states and cities such as Bavaria, Saxony, and Zurich, banned tobacco in the 17th century; in 1633, the Sultan Murad IV ordered the death penalty for smoking in Constantinople (now Istanbul, Turkey), but "even the fear of death was of no avail with the passionate devotees of the habit," one historian wrote. Severe punishments including torture were proclaimed in Russia in 1634 by the tsar, Michael Romanov. In Japan, where smoking was banned in 1603, the mere cultivation of tobacco was made a crime. But smokers could still be found — even among the emperor's entourage. By 1625, permission again was granted to grow tobacco, and the plant soon became a fixture of Japanese society.

Modern Efforts to Ban Tobacco

The early 1900s witnessed the growing popularity of a new smoking product — cigarettes, which were mass produced and which soon surpassed cigars, pipes, chewing tobacco, and snuff as the most popular way to get nicotine into the body. In particular, the development of a milder type of tobacco, known as "Virginia," which made cigarette smoke easier to inhale, helped popularize cigarettes among women and teenagers — even among children. Heavy advertising and promotion campaigns, including even the use of souvenir baseball cards and buttons featuring well-known cartoon characters, also encouraged youngsters to try cigarettes.

The rise of cigarette smoking by women and children prompted the establishment of anticigarette groups similar to the antisaloon leagues. Efforts to ban smoking resulted in cigarette prohibition laws in 14 states by 1921, the year after alcohol prohibition took effect. The immediate failure of these laws was even more apparent than the failure of Prohibition, and by 1927 all of them had been repealed.

Other laws regarding cigarettes remained in effect, however, as many do today. Thirty-eight states now restrict the sale or distribution of tobacco products to minors. The minimum age at which youths can legally buy tobacco products

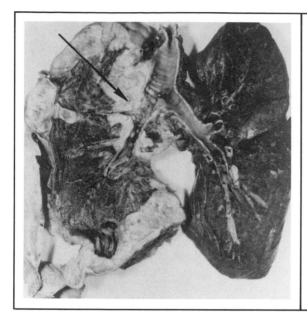

The cancerous lung of a heavy smoker. Although cigarettes had long been considered harmful, it was not until 1964 that the U.S. Surgeon General reported that a direct link had been made between smoking and lung cancer.

ranges from 15 to 19. The laws of 14 states allow those under the age of 18 to buy tobacco, and in 12 states, no laws at all deal with the sale or distribution of tobacco to minors.

Although the harmful physical effects of smoking have long been known — an old nickname for cigarettes was "coffin nails" — it was not until the release of the U.S. Surgeon General's Report in January 1964 that a direct link between cigarette smoking and lung cancer was made. Although the tobacco companies continue to contend that the scientific evidence regarding smoking and disease is inconclusive, the case linking smoking tobacco to not only cancer but heart disease is all but proven.

Partly for this reason, the nationwide antismoking movement has grown progressively stronger in recent years. Such campaigns, which include legally mandated educational programs in elementary and secondary schools, have publicized medical evidence of the dangers of smoking and have helped change the image of smoking from that of a chic and sophisticated habit to one that is self-abusive and unhealthy.

In addition, many antismoking groups have changed their focus. Rather than calling for outright bans on cigarettes and other tobacco, these groups are now urging restrictions on where and when people can smoke, how tobacco can be advertised, and to whom it can be sold. This strategy has met with considerable success. A survey by the U.S. Department of Health and Human Services found nearly 400 state laws dealing with smoking and health, including laws requiring money obtained from taxing the sale of tobacco to be earmarked for special health-related programs and research. All 50 states and the District of Columbia regulate the sale and/or use of tobacco in some way. Forty-two states and the District of Columbia have passed laws restricting smoking in public places; 33 states ban smoking on buses, subways, or streetcars; 17 states and the District of Columbia restrict smoking in government and/or private workplaces; and smoking in school buildings and on school grounds is regulated in 27 states. Only eight states do not restrict smoking in public places.

San Francisco mayor Dianne Feinstein signed into effect the ordinance that regulated smoking in private offices in the city in 1983. Behind the mayor is Wendy Nelder, Board of Supervisors president and author of the ordinance.

The toughest antismoking laws probably are those in Minnesota, Montana, Nebraska, and Utah, where smoking is banned practically everywhere except outdoors and in private homes. By contrast, 11 states — some of them with important tobacco-growing industries — have no major antismoking laws. These states are Virginia, West Virginia, North Carolina, South Carolina, Alabama, Louisiana, Mississippi, Tennessee, Illinois, Indiana, and Wyoming.

In February 1987, the federal government restricted smoking among 890,000 federal workers in 6,800 federal buildings; in May 1987, New York State passed a rule forbidding smoking in most areas of public buildings, including stores, banks, schools, hospitals, and offices, as well as in taxis and limousines. (The rule did not ultimately become the law because of a minor technicality, but it is noteworthy that these restrictions were drafted in the first place.) In Texas, 14 cities and towns now have antismoking ordinances; in California, state law regulates smoking in supermarkets, health facilities, public meetings, and parts of public buildings. At least 112 California cities and counties regulate smoking in private workplaces; 113 require nonsmoking sections in restaurants, and 99 restrict smoking in retail stores. Citing the health hazards to nonsmokers of breathing the tobacco smoke exhaled by smokers — so-called passive smoking — a group called Americans for Nonsmokers' Rights based in Berkeley, California, has drafted a model smoking-pollution control law, which it provides to municipalities around the country that are considering such an action. Although the group has not succeeded in getting this law past the Berkeley City Council, its spirit is increasingly taking hold throughout the country.

Just as the state laws regulating smoking vary, so do the penalties for violating them. Most states impose small fines for smoking infractions, ranging from $1 in West Virginia to $25 in Connecticut, Delaware, Kansas, Pennsylvania, and Vermont. Fines of $100 and $300 are imposed in Alaska, Maryland, New Jersey, and the District of Columbia for those who break the laws restricting smoking in public places. The laws that regulate the selling or furnishing of tobacco products to minors also vary; in Kansas, those convicted of selling cigarettes to minors must either pay a $1,000 fine, serve up to one year in prison, or both.

Putting the Brake on Cigarette Ads

As the American Cancer Society has noted, cigarettes are the nation's most heavily advertised consumer product. Believe it or not, about 50 years ago some cigarette advertisements claimed that their products were actually *healthy*; in November 1936, one magazine contained an advertisement for Camel cigarettes that urged people to smoke a Camel after *every course* of their Thanksgiving dinner as a way to improve their digestion. Celebrity endorsements were also important in tobacco advertising. A 1951 magazine advertisement for Chesterfield cigarettes featured Ronald Reagan, then a Hollywood star, saying he was sending a carton of his favorite cigarettes to all his friends for Christmas. He also posed in advertisements promoting cigars. Mr. Reagan's well-known fondness for jelly beans today stems from his successful effort later to quit smoking.

In addition to these magazine advertisements, there was a time when both radio and television broadcast commercials touting the virtues of a particular brand. In 1970, however, Congress passed a law banning broadcast advertising of cigarettes after January 1, 1971. Since then, cigarette companies have increased their magazine, newspaper, and billboard advertising more than threefold. In 1985, more than $2 billion was spent on such ads, with pictures of good-looking, prosperous young men and women enjoying themselves, cigarettes in hand or dangling from their lips, as they relax in scenic surroundings, engage in healthy outdoor activities, or savor good food and drink.

Such antismoking advocates as the American Medical Association and the American Cancer Society have urged Congress to ban all cigarette advertising and promotions, including newspaper and magazine ads, billboard ads, and the sponsorship of sporting events and concerts. A bill to ban all print advertising of cigarettes was introduced in Congress in 1987 but did not pass. The tobacco industry says that similar bans and restrictions on advertising in Spain, France, Finland, Norway, Sweden, East Germany, and the Sudan have not really cut down on smoking in these countries, and advocates of free speech such as the American Civil Liberties Union (ACLU) contend that such a law here would be unconsti-

A 1929 advertisement for Lucky Strike cigarettes features actress Constance Talmadge. Early cigarette ads often included celebrity endorsements that made false claims.

tutional. As long as cigarettes are legal, they argue, a complete ban on advertising them would violate the First Amendment's guarantee of free speech.

Other civil libertarians argue, however, that tobacco advertising is inherently misleading and promotes a substance that is known to be hazardous, so the Constitution's free speech protection would not apply to these advertisements. In Canada, the government agreed with those who call for a ban on all tobacco advertising. It announced in April 1987 that all tobacco advertisements and most promotional activities sponsored by tobacco firms would be banned there by the beginning of 1989.

Although it has not yet banned all cigarette advertisements, Congress is considering doubling the tax on a pack of cigarettes from 16 cents to 32 cents, hoping that the increase will deter many teenagers from either starting or continuing to smoke. In 1984 it passed a law requiring stronger and more prominent health warnings on all cigarette packs, advertisements, and billboards. Among the new warnings,

Congress has acted. The next step is yours.

Caution: Cigarette smoking may be hazardous to your health

An early warning notice on cigarette packages cautioned that smoking could be hazardous to health. Although current cigarette warnings are far more detailed in their listings of health hazards, many cigarette manufacturers maintain that the scientific evidence backing these claims is inconclusive.

which are 50% larger than before, are those that say "Warning: Smoking causes lung cancer, heart disease, and emphysema and may complicate pregnancy," and "Smoking by pregnant women may result in fetal injury, premature birth, and low birth weight."

Ironically, although the tobacco industry initially opposed the placement of warnings on cigarette packs in 1965, it has been able to cite those warnings as a defense in lawsuits filed by the families of smokers who have died from smoking-related illnesses, seeking damages from the cigarette companies. Federal courts in Boston, Atlanta, and Philadelphia have ruled in separate cases that the congressionally imposed warnings about cigarettes preempt state laws regarding product liability, the responsibility the manufacturer of a product has for injuries consumers may get from using it.

The Growing Opposition to Smoking

All of the new laws and regulations restricting where people can smoke, the heightened warnings about the ill effects of tobacco products, and the increased interest Americans have in physical fitness and healthy living have combined to change the public mood regarding cigarette smoking. Many people no longer consider it fashionable to smoke, and the percentage of cigarette smokers among the adult U.S. population has dropped dramatically. The U.S. Department of Health and Human Services says the most significant decline in the percentage of current cigarette smokers occurred among men, of whom 52.9% were smokers in 1965 but less than 33% smoke today, probably the lowest level of cigarette smoking among men since before World War I. There has also been a decline in cigarette smoking among adult women since the 1960s, but it has been less impressive. In 1965, 34.1% of adult women smoked; today approximately 28% do.

According to surveys of high school seniors conducted by the National Institute of Drug Abuse, cigarette smoking among teenagers has declined sharply since 1977, although female teenagers also continue to smoke more than the males. Ten years ago, 30% of female high school seniors smoked; by 1984, according to the latest figures, only 20% smoked. In 1977, approximately 26.5% of male high school seniors smoked; by 1984, only 16% did.

In 1984, Dr. C. Everett Koop, the U.S. surgeon general, joined with the American Cancer Society in calling for a "smoke-free society" by the year 2000. Public opinion surveys show that smoking is becoming more and more unpopular; according to one recent Gallup poll, 79% of all Americans — including 76% of the smokers — believe that smoking should be restricted in the workplace. Another survey by the American Lung Association shows that 9 out of 10 current smokers wish they could quit. No doubt, like Mark Twain, many of them have done so many times already.

METCALF'S COCA WINE

From Fresh Coca Leaves.

A Pleasant Tonic and Invigorator.

COCA LEAVES have been in use by the native Indians in South America from the earliest times as a remedy for every malady, from a simple cut to neuralgia and headache ; and while chewing it, they pass whole days in traveling or working without food, eating heartily in the evening, without inconvenience, and passing the night in refreshing sleep.

COCA LEAVES have been recommended by Ringer as valuable in *Febrile Disorders*, by restraining tissue metamorphosis, and for the same reason in Phthisis.

With decided anodyne and antispasmodic qualities, they have been employed in Typhus, *Scorbutus*, Gastralgia, Anæmia, Enteralgia, and to assist digestion.

Dose of Wine of Coca.—One-half to one wineglassful three times daily.

An 1889 advertisement for Metcalf's Coca Wine, the active ingredient of which was cocaine. Many drugs, including both cocaine and heroin, were once available over-the-counter in various elixirs and cure-alls.

CHAPTER 3

ONCE LEGAL, NOW OUTLAWED: THE EVOLUTION OF ILLICIT-DRUG LAWS

Sherlock Holmes took his bottle from the corner of the mantelpiece, and his hypodermic syringe from its neat morocco [leather] case. With his long, white, nervous fingers he adjusted the needle, and rolled back his left shirt cuff . . .; he thrust the sharp point home, pressed down the tiny piston, and sank back into the velvet-lined arm-chair with a long sigh of satisfaction. "What is it today . . . [Dr. Watson asked], "morphine or cocaine?"
— Sir Arthur Conan Doyle, *The Sign of the Four.*

All of the drugs that are currently illegal were once, like alcohol and tobacco, perfectly legal to use — and in some cases even less restricted than alcohol and tobacco are today. Morphine, heroin, cocaine, marijuana, and hallucinogens (such as LSD) were often freely manufactured and promoted as beneficial wonder drugs. By the beginning of the 20th century, however, the bad effects that these drugs could have on people both physically and mentally became a growing cause of concern, not just in the United States but in Europe and Asia as well.

During the 1800s, the trade and sale of opium, the dried juice of the unripe opium poppy, was extensive here and abroad. In the view of some historians, it "was the world's most valuable single commodity trade of the nineteeth century." The biggest market for the drug was China, to which Great Britain sold hundreds of thousands of pounds per year of opium obtained in India. The emperor of China recognized that the drug was harming his subjects and tried to stop its importation, but the business was so valuable that Great Britain actually went to war with China twice — once between 1839 and 1842, and again between 1856 and 1858 — in order to force the Chinese to allow the continuation of the opium trade.

The chief active ingredient in opium is morphine, which from the mid-19th to early 20th century was commonly used as a painkiller and a sedative, as well as for coughs, diarrhea, and other ailments. (On occasion it still is used today as a painkiller in terminal cancer cases.) Like opium, morphine was used in many 19th-century patent medicines, which were available in drug stores and groceries, or through mail order

Chinese commissioner Chin orders the destruction of opium chests belonging to British merchants, an action that eventually led to the Opium Wars (1839–42 and 1856–58).

A group of wounded Civil War soldiers at Savage Station, Virginia, in 1862. Morphine was so widely used to treat wounded soldiers during the Civil War that addiction to it became known as the "soldier's disease."

firms to anyone who wanted them. Morphine use became especially common during the Civil War (1861–65), when military doctors gave it to wounded soldiers to ease their pain. So many soldiers became dependent on morphine that addiction to it was known as "the soldier's disease." In England, women factory workers even gave laudanum — which is a concoction of opium and alcohol — to their crying infants to quiet them. Writers used it as well. In England, the novelist Charles Dickens, the mystery writer Wilkie Collins, and the Romantic poet Samuel Coleridge used opium. In the United States, the poet and short-story writer poet Edgar Allan Poe used it too.

Another drug readily available in the 19th century was cocaine, which, like morphine, was used by some prominent members of society. Cocaine was in fact part of the original formula for Coca-Cola, created in 1886 by Dr. J. C. Pemberton as a non-alcoholic "temperance" drink composed of cola nuts, caramel, and coca leaves — which contain cocaine. Cocaine remained part of the Coca-Cola formula until 1903, when it was replaced by caffeine. Another well-known tonic mixture of the time was Vin Mariani, invented by an Italian named

Angelo Mariani, who used cocaine as a main ingredient in his brew. He managed to obtain testimonials for it from European nobility, famous writers, politicians, and other prominent people. Pope Leo XIII even gave Mariani a gold medal in 1898. The author Robert Louis Stevenson supposedly used cocaine in an undiluted form, and he purportedly wrote the classic tale *The Strange Case of Dr. Jekyll and Mr. Hyde* while under the influence of the drug. And, as the quotation at the beginning of this chapter shows, fiction's most famous detective, Sherlock Holmes, used morphine and cocaine — perhaps because his creator, the British author and physician Sir Arthur Conan Doyle, also used cocaine.

In the Sherlock Holmes stories, however, Holmes's well-known partner in crime detection, Dr. Watson, vigorously disapproved of his friend's use of drugs, for as Conan Doyle knew, addiction to cocaine and morphine was considered

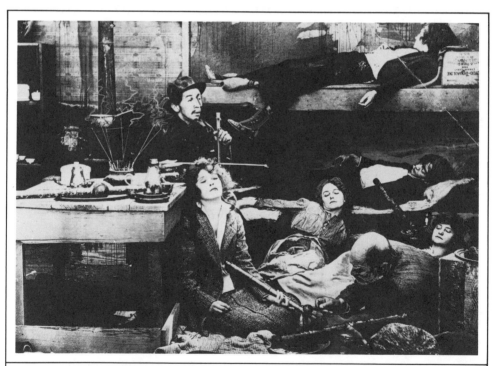

Opium dens, such as this one in New York City, were quite popular in the United States during the early 1900s.

disreputable, not only in Great Britain but in the United States as well. The mother of the famous playwright Eugene O'Neill became hopelessly addicted to morphine because a careless doctor gave it to her during an illness, a sad event that O'Neill wrote about in his moving play *A Long Day's Journey into Night*. O'Neill considered the painful story of his mother's drug addiction so shameful, however, that he would not allow the play to be performed during his lifetime. Similarly, Dr. William Stewart Halsted, one of the founding physicians of the Johns Hopkins Hospital and Medical School, and among the world's greatest surgeons in the late 19th and early 20th centuries, sought to test the pain-killing effects of cocaine by injecting himself with it. He became dependent on cocaine and was able to break the addiction only by switching to morphine — an addiction that was kept secret until 1969, 47 years after Halsted's death in 1922.

The problem of addiction to these drugs was evident not only to private citizens but to local and state goverments as well. Unfortunately, actions to control the problem were not entirely successful. For example, a number of cities and states passed laws to ban the smoking of opium (the first of these was a San Francisco ordinance in 1875), but they were largely ineffective. During the 19th century, the annual consumption in the United States of opium and its derivatives (such as heroin) rose from an average of about 12 grains per person a year in 1840 — with one grain being the average single dose — to 52 grains per person per year by the mid-1890s. By 1900, the number of people in the United States who were addicted to opiates was probably close to 250,000 out of a population of 76 million — or almost 3% of the population — a percentage that has never been equalled or surpassed since. If that were the rate of addiction today, there would be 1.1 million addicts in the United States, or about twice the current official estimate.

The extent of drug addiction in the country, as well as revelations about phony medical cures, prompted the development of a nationwide reform movement aimed at cleaning up the food and medical industries. It had the support of President Theodore Roosevelt and resulted in the passage of the Pure Food and Drug Act of 1906, which was this country's first real consumer protection law. Among other things, the law required the manufacturers of medicines that contained opium, morphine, or other drugs, specifically to say so on their labels. Later on, the law was amended to require that the exact amount of each drug in a medicine be put on the label, and that the opium or morphine used in a medicine meet the standards of purity set by the government. In 1906, Congress passed the Narcotic Drug Importation Act and the Opium Exclusion Act, aimed at controlling the amount of opium and morphine brought into this country. (A national law banning the domestic growth of the opium poppy was not passed until 1942.)

Trying to Stem the Opium Trade

The increasing determination in the United States to curb opiate abuse at home went hand in hand with a growing disapproval of Great Britain's continuing opium trade with China. Many people, in the United States and elsewhere, believed that this trade was destroying the Chinese people. Traders in other goods also complained that the money China was wasting on drugs could be better spent on the products they had to sell. In 1909, Theodore Roosevelt issued a call for an international conference in Shanghai, China, to address the opium issue. In 1911, a second international conference at the Hague in the Netherlands produced a treaty known as The Hague Convention of 1912, which was signed by 34 nations and sought to control narcotics manufacturing and trafficking worldwide.

In order to enable the United States to do its part in enforcing the Hague Treaty, Congress passed the Harrison Narcotic Act of 1914, which was the nation's first law aimed at controlling drug use. The Harrison Act said that the manufacturers and importers of narcotics, and the pharmacists and physicians who prescribed them, had to be licensed to do so. In some ways the law seemed to be only a means of controlling the lawful marketing of narcotics, but it was really designed to stamp out the use of these drugs altogether. A section of the law dealing with doctors said they could prescribe narcotics "in the course of [their] professional practice only." Because narcotics addiction was not classified as an illness, addicts were not considered patients and doctors therefore could not prescribe narcotics to addicts as part of their medical practice.

A U.S. Narcotic Division officer examines a can of opium confiscated in 1926. The Harrison Narcotic Act of 1914 was the first U.S. law regulating such drugs as heroin and opium.

Ironically, the Harrison Act, the first American law restricting the use of psychoactive drugs, did not originally have provisions concerning two of the most abused substances in the world today: heroin and marijuana. The reason heroin was not initially restricted was that this morphine derivative, which was discovered in 1898, was not thought to be addictive and actually was recommended as a substitute for morphine. It was also considered an excellent medicine for coughs, asthma, bronchitis, tuberculosis, and other lung diseases. Heroin was first sold as a medicine by the Bayer Company of Germany, the company that also first marketed aspirin. (The Bayer Company lost the patent rights to both aspirin and heroin when Germany lost World War I.)

Despite initial hopes for heroin, its addictive quality soon became apparent. The American Medical Association warned about it as early as 1902. But it was only after the banning of morphine and cocaine when heroin became the most popular

"recreational" drug, that the upsurge in its use led to calls
for its prohibition, especially after law enforcement officials
in the early 1920s determined that heroin users were responsible for many violent crimes. Congress responded to
the reported heroin problem in 1924 by adding it to the list
of drugs banned by the Harrison Act. The 1924 law forbade
the importation of heroin even for medicinal purposes, and
later banned domestic production of it as well.

Marijuana was not initially included in the Harrison Act,
either. This drug was probably introduced into the United
States around 1910, when Mexican migrant workers carried
it across the border. It became popular during the following
decade, when jazz musicians and their followers began using
marijuana regularly. During the Prohibition era, people went
to so-called "tea pads," which were like speakeasies or opium
dens, to smoke marijuana. Many people, however, associated
marijuana use with violent behavior in Mexico as well as in
parts of the United States. Partially in response to this sen-
timent, Congress passed the Marijuana Tax Act of 1937, an
unusual law that made it illegal to sell, barter, or even give
away marijuana without a stamp permit and proper tax
stamps. (Medical use of marijuana was permitted under the
law.) The states also passed anti-marijuana laws, some of them
with extremely severe penalties. In Louisiana, for example,
the law allowed a judge to sentence someone to 30 years at
hard labor or even to death for selling marijuana to anyone
under 21 years of age — although no one there or anywhere
else in the United States was ever sentenced to death in a
marijuana case.

Despite the harsh laws, the popularity of marijuana grew,
especially in the mid-to-late 1960s, a time when defiance of
conventional values and norms was common among America's young people. Arrests for marijuana possession sky-
rocketed. In California, for example, 7,560 marijuana arrests
were reported statewide in 1964; by 1968, California police
reported arresting 50,327 people on marijuana charges. By
1969, the federal government estimated that between 8 million and 12 million Americans had tried marijuana at least
once; that about 25% of them, or some 2 million to 3 million
people, were using it whenever it happened to be available;
and that about 10%, or 800 thousand to 1.2 million, were

using it every day. Other drug use, particularly of heroin, also increased in the late 1960s and early 1970s. Thousands of young American servicemen became addicted to heroin in Vietnam, where it was cheap and easy to get.

For some years, the federal government tried to beef up the Harrison Act, in the process passing no fewer than 55 laws to supplement that original antidrug statute. The penalties were increased for dealing in or possessing drugs. New drugs, such as the hallucinogens LSD (Lysergic acid diethylamide) and PCP (Phencylidine, popularly called "angel dust") were made illegal, and restrictions were placed on the sale and distribution of depressants such as barbiturates.

In 1970, Congress passed the Comprehensive Drug Abuse Prevention and Control Act, a law that has consolidated all the previous measures. Under this law, as under earlier statutes, mere possession of a prohibited drug is illegal — and in order for someone to be found guilty of "possessing" an illegal drug, it is not necessary for the police to prove that a person had actual possession of it, say, in a pocket or a purse. Under the law, it is possible for several people to have "constructive" or "joint" possession of an illegal thing. "Constructive" possession occurs when several people knowingly possess an illegal substance and can lay claim to it together, even if none of them is actually holding the substance when the arrest is made. "Joint" possession occurs when one member of a group has an illegal drug in his or her physical possession or control with the knowledge and consent of the others, all of whom are in the company of the person who actually has the drug. For example, if five or six people are sitting in a car from which marijuana smoke is coming, all of them could be found guilty of possessing the marijuana, because each of them presumably knew that marijuana was being illegally smoked in the car, and each of them "controlled" enough of it to be able to take a single puff on one marijuana cigarette while they were in the car.

As part of the 1970 law, Congress created five "schedules" to classify illegal drugs according to what the legislators considered a drug's potential for abuse; whether it has any use in medicine; and whether it is likely to cause "user-dependency." Schedule I drugs have no recognized medical use and a high potential for abuse. These include hallucinogens such as LSD; opiates that have no legal medical use, such as heroin; and marijuana and hashish, which is the dried resin given off by the marijuana plant and more potent than its leaves. Schedule II contains cocaine; opiates that have recognized medical uses, such as morphine and codeine; and some amphetamines and barbiturates. Schedule III drugs have a lower potential for abuse and may be prescribed at a doctor's discretion. Non-narcotic painkillers and drugs such as Valium are in Schedule IV. Their use must be prescribed by a doctor. Schedule V includes mixtures and compounds containing small amounts of narcotics, such as codeine-containing prescription cough medicines.

The Billion-Dollar War on Drugs

Illegal drug use remained a major law-enforcement problem despite the consolidated, comprehensive narcotics law. After Ronald Reagan became president in January 1981, he said his administration planned to launch a mammoth attack on organized crime and drug dealing. In terms of the money spent on enforcing the anti-drug abuse laws, that pledge has been fulfilled — even though the success of the effort has been mixed and the funding for it may now be cut.

The Reagan administration says that it has expanded the enforcement of federal drug laws to its greatest level in history. The federal budget for drug law enforcement was more than $1.2 billion in 1985, a 75% increase over the money spent on it in 1981. In 1987, funding to enforce the drug laws reached $3.9 billion. Of that huge sum, $1.37 billion was earmarked for intercepting and seizing illegally smuggled heroin, cocaine, and marijuana. In 1986, drug agents succeeded in seizing 27 tons of cocaine, 1,106 tons of marijuana, 9 tons of hashish, and large amounts of heroin on its way into the United States — but that was merely a fraction of what did get in, according to the General Accounting Office (GAO), which monitors federal spending for Congress. The GAO estimated that 138 tons of cocaine, 11,000 tons of marijuana, 7 tons of heroin, and 165 tons of hashish slipped through the law enforcement network set up along the nation's borders. The size of our borders and the ingenuity of the smugglers make the drug agents' task very difficult, especially along the long, southern coastal region, with its remote and intricate waterways.

Efforts have been undertaken to bolster the federal Drug Enforcement Administration, the agency that oversees the investigation of federal drug crimes. The Federal Bureau of Investigation (FBI), the Defense Department, the Coast Guard, the Internal Revenue Service (IRS), the Customs Service, the Bureau of Alcohol, Tobacco and Firearms, and the U.S. Marshal's Office have been added to the federal government's anti-drug forces or have beefed up their own existing anti-drug campaigns. Some new operations, such as the Organized Crime Drug Enforcement Task Force, which has centers in 13 major cities, have been created in an attempt to coordinate all of these law-enforcement activities.

In all, 14 federal agencies now are engaged in combating the smuggling, corruption, tax evasion, money laundering, racketeering, and violence that are part of the illegal drug business. In addition, the president has authorized the U.S. foreign intelligence operations (such as the Central Intelligence Agency) and military services to uncover information on drug trafficking.

An undercover narcotics agent, her face covered to conceal her identity, testifies before the House Crime Committee in 1972. The committee was investigating drug abuse in the public schools.

U.S. Customs agents confiscated 910 pounds of cocaine in this 1984 drug bust off the coast of Florida. As part of improved law enforcement, drug agents seized more than 27 tons of cocaine in 1986 alone.

The centerpiece of the federal government's intensified attack on narcotics is the Anti-Drug Abuse Act of 1986, which has kept the "schedules" of the 1970 anti-drug law but has greatly increased the penalties for possession and trafficking in illegal drugs, and has ended the possibility of suspended sentences, probation, or parole in most cases.

In the 1970s, the tremendous rise in the use of marijuana prompted the growth of a movement to legalize it. Between 1973 and 1978, 11 states passed laws that "decriminalized" marijuana, making possession of small amounts of it for personal use a civil but not a criminal offense, punishable only by a fine of as little as $100. But possessing marijuana — or growing it — still remains against the law, even in those 11 states: Oregon, Alaska, Maine, Colorado, California, Ohio, Minnesota, North Carolina, New York and Nebraska. Since 1978, however, no other states have decriminalized the possession of marijuana, much less made it legal to have or sell.

In fact, the public mood seems to be turning the other way. For example, a 1979 poll in California indicated that 42% of the adults surveyed thought marijuana should be legalized. But when a petition was circulated in 1980 to put the legalization of marijuana on the ballot for a vote, it was unsuccessful. In 1986, Oregon voters rejected a proposition that would have made it legal for people 18 years of age or older to grow and possess marijuana for their own use. The President's Commission on Organized Crime has urged re-criminalization of the marijuana laws in the 11 states that decriminalized marijuana possession 10 years ago. (That seems unlikely to happen, however.) Evidence also exists that marijuana has some medical value, and 33 states authorize its use for the treatment of glaucoma, an eye disease.

A young woman harvests opium poppies in Burma. Official efforts to curtail the cultivation of such crops have not met with much success because growers are unwilling to relinquish their high profits.

CHAPTER 4

THE WORLDWIDE BATTLE AGAINST DRUGS

Ever since the multinational conferences in Shanghai, China, in 1909 and The Hague in the Netherlands in 1911, countries around the world have tried to control the spread of illicit drug trafficking and use. By and large, the nations have concentrated their law-enforcement efforts within their own borders. But during the past 40 years, a number of international treaties have been signed and programs begun to try to stop the worldwide explosion of the drug problem.

In 1948, a United Nations treaty was signed to control synthetic drugs such as methadone, which was created during World War II as a substitute for morphine, and barbiturates. Two more recent agreements sponsored by the United Nations are designed to regulate the international drug trade. In 1961, the so-called Single Convention on Narcotic Drugs was devised to replace the Hague treaty of 1912 and all the later international agreements on drugs. It created new controls over opium and its derivatives, such as heroin and morphine, as well as other drugs that generally are illegal, such as cocaine, marijuana and, unless governmentally distributed, methadone. Ten years later, the Convention on Psychotropic Substances of 1971 created similar controls over many new

Armed Colombian soldiers prepare to battle leftist guerrillas, who were backed by local drug traffickers. The guerrillas, who laid siege to the Palace of Justice in 1985, eventually killed 12 justices of the court.

synthetic drugs, such as hallucinogens, stimulants, sedatives, and tranquilizers. The 115 nations that have signed these agreements promise to impose tough controls on the production, manufacture, availability, and distribution of these drugs, both for scientific use within the countries themselves and for export. The United Nations also has created a Commission on Narcotic Drugs, which oversees the enforcement of the treaties to curb drug trading and use. In addition, a European Council serves as the chief body for coordinating the battle against drug abuse and dealing there, and law-enforcement cooperation also is provided by the International Criminal Police Organization (Interpol) and the Customs Cooperation Council. Proposals have also been made to classify drug trafficking as an international crime so that it can be prosecuted anywhere in the world without regard to where the illegal drugs were produced or sold.

Despite these international agreements and cooperative efforts, many of the countries that have signed the treaties — particularly the nations where much of the heroin, cocaine, and marijuana is grown — have great difficulty preventing the production and trafficking in illegal drugs. Efforts to stop farmers from growing the plants that produce illegal drugs, such as the opium poppy, which is turned into heroin, and the coca plant, which provides cocaine, have not been effective. The programs aimed at wiping out illegal plants and encouraging farmers to grow substitute crops, such as coffee, bananas, potatoes, or rice, have also been largely useless. The illegal plants are easier to grow and promise 10 to 20 times as much profit as the legal crops. Indeed, some local leaders in the remote areas where the illegal crops grow actually threaten farmers if they *do not* raise coca plants or opium poppies, both of which are crucial to the economies of these countries. (Nor have U.S. crop substitution programs met with any real success. The U.S. can offer farmers only $140 per acre to grow crops other than the coca plant, whereas growing coca on that same acre can earn between $2,000 and $4,000.)

In addition, the Latin American nations that produce almost all of the world's cocaine, much of its marijuana, and a good deal of its heroin have traditionally resisted attempts made by the United States to intervene in their domestic affairs. Despite some efforts at cooperation, the Latin American countries are basically reluctant to allow U.S. narcotics agents or military forces to be involved in crackdowns on the production centers for cocaine and other illegal drugs. A possible reason for this reluctance is that whether these countries like to admit it or not, they desperately need the money the illegal narcotics trade provides.

Narcotics dealers also have great power in the countries where illegal drugs are produced. They actually rule entire areas of some nations and control many police chiefs, judges, military leaders, and politicians through bribery and intimidation. In Colombia, for example, commandos backed by drug dealers attacked the Palace of Justice in November 1985, while that country's Supreme Court was in the process of ordering local drug traffickers sent to the United States to be jailed. Twelve justices of the court were killed and in the ensuing battle to recapture the court building more than 100 people lost their lives. It is estimated that at least 200 Colombian national policemen have been fired because of the part they have played in illegal drug dealings, and some 400 local judges are suspected of corruption. Colombian drug dealers own soccer teams, zoos, and public housing projects, and they spend an estimated $115 million a year to bribe officials and police.

In Bolivia, a general who overthrew the government in 1980 — in what was called the Cocaine Coup — released leading drug dealers from prison and ordered police records about them destroyed. Although Bolivian democracy was restored in 1982, the campaign to combat drug dealing remains a tough one, and the military there is still corrupt. It is estimated that Bolivia earned $600 million from cocaine trafficking in 1986. It would take $100 million in U.S. aid to begin replacing that income.

Another South American country plagued by military and police corruption arising from illegal drug dealings is Peru. In 1985, 100 air force personnel, more than 200 top police officers, and more than 1,000 policemen in that country were tried for corruption, and several hundred judges have been

An artist's rendering of the 1986–87 "Pizza Connection" trial. During the trial it was revealed that the Mafia distributed approximately $1.6 billion worth of heroin within the United States between 1979 and 1984.

A custom-made car used by Corsican narcotics traffickers to smuggle 246 pounds of heroin into the United States. The car was seized by Federal authorities at a New York pier in 1967.

investigated. "Like governments in other drug producing countries, the Peruvian government is virtually impotent in the face of the massive profits to be made from drug trading," wrote Brian Freemantle.

Countries that serve as the main processing and distribution places for illegal drugs also have severe law-enforcement problems. In Italy, for example, a total of 400 years in prison sentences was imposed on 65 members of three drug-dealing, Mafia "families" in Palermo, Sicily, in 1983. Mafia gunmen had ambushed judges, police chiefs, and other officials involved in the arrests and sentencing, killing them with bursts of machine gun fire. Perhaps the most famous European drug-dealing operation was the "French Connection," the subject of both a book and a movie. It was a conspiracy involving an international cast of drug dealers who shipped tons of heroin from Marseilles, France, to New York until police cracked the operation in the early 1970s. A similar French-connected drug ring was broken in late 1985. Despite these arrests, the illegal drug trade remains a big business and is often the cause of violent dealings; for example, the battles between French gangsters in Marseilles over the narcotics business in which they compete has led to more than 20 murders in recent years. The French government has sought to toughen enforcement of its domestic drug laws, rejecting any suggestions that it decriminalize the use of "soft drugs," such as marijuana. Instead, it has increased police efforts to combat drug abuse.

Addiction: Crime or Disease?

Naturally, foreign countries have problems with drug addiction, too, and deal with it as best they can. In Japan, for example, the first antidrug law, which was passed in 1870, required the beheading by sword of all traffickers, and it is still possible to be sentenced to life in prison there for dealing in heroin. Under Japanese law, the user of an illegal drug is considered as bad as the supplier, since the user creates the demand for the drug. Great Britain, on the other hand, considers drug addiction a medical rather than a criminal issue and has far more lenient policies regarding substance abuse than Japan does.

Patients await their daily dose of methadone at a methadone clinic in New York City. The adoption of methadone maintenance in the United States paralleled the British practice of supplying addicts with heroin.

As in the United States, heroin, cocaine, and other now-illegal drugs were readily available in Great Britain in the late 19th century. In fact, a British government commission in 1893 flatly declared that there was no danger at all in using opium. Gradually, the British view on drugs changed, however, especially following the international conferences in the early 20th century, which called for curbs on drug trafficking. In 1920, the British Parliament passed its first Dangerous Drugs Act, and in 1921 it established Dangerous Drugs Regulations, which were aimed at keeping the distribution of opiates within the hands of the medical profession. Three years later, another government commission studied law enforcement efforts in other countries — particularly the laws in the United States that banned the distribution of opium, morphine, and heroin to narcotics addicts. It decided instead that drug addiction in Great Britain should be regarded as an illness that doctors could treat by prescribing morphine and heroin for the addicts. A new set of Dangerous Drugs Regulations were created in 1926 to carry out this policy.

For about 30 years this British system seemed to work well. Under it, addicts never had an automatic right to heroin or other drugs. The treatment they received and the amount and sort of drug supplied to them was a determination left to the doctor, who could decide whether to treat the addict by supplying drugs; reduce the addict's dependency on drugs by reducing the supply of them gradually; or have the addict immediately refrain from drug use — go "cold turkey" — by cutting off all supply of drugs. According to official British statistics, by 1951 there were only 301 addicts in the entire country who were known to be receiving narcotics from a doctor. But a few years later, the British government abolished the professional panels of doctors who oversaw the prescribing of drugs by physicians, and within a few more years a number of doctors began to over-prescribe narcotics in the mistaken belief that they were preventing the creation of an illegal black market for drugs by giving addicts all the narcotics they needed — and more. In actuality, the doctors helped create a black market for drugs, since the addicts began selling the narcotics they did not use.

Throughout the 1960s and 1970s, the number of drug addicts in Great Britain grew. In 1966, the ability to prescribe heroin was taken away from the average doctor and given only to physicians and clinics licensed to do so. In 1971, a much tougher Misuse of Drugs Act was passed. It created the requirement for a special license to produce, possess, or supply LSD, marijuana, or other drugs with no established medical use, as well as for cocaine and heroin used for purposes other than medical treatment. The law put different narcotics into three categories — A to C — that are similar to the drug schedules in the United States. Class A drugs in England are what authorities there consider the most dangerous substances, including heroin, cocaine, methadone, marijuana, LSD, injectable amphetamines, and opium. Under a 1985 law, the maximum sentence for illegally trafficking in these drugs is life imprisonment.

The drug problem in Great Britain remains serious. It is estimated that there are now 150,000 users of cocaine, marijuana, and other illegal drugs, as well as some 66,000 heroin addicts who are getting their drugs from sources other than treatment centers. The continuing growth of the black market for drugs in Great Britain has prompted a gradual change in the attitude of many doctors and law enforcement officials there. Many now believe that the policy of providing addicts with a sufficient amount of heroin or methadone to maintain their habit is "not an acceptable medical response to drug abuse," according to a British government booklet on the problem. Many of the clinics that treat addicts by giving them drugs are now switching their procedure from one of prescribing "maintenance doses" of narcotics indefinitely to one of giving addicts gradually reduced doses of narcotics, particularly methadone, in an effort to curb their addiction and eventually "detoxify" them.

Despite the new toughness of the "British approach" to drug addiction, the different drug-treatment clinics around Great Britain vary their procedures greatly regarding the amounts of drugs addicts receive and how long the prescription period lasts. The British government also continues to expand the number of drug treatment facilities around the country.

Adopting the "British Approach"

Other countries have considered adopting the "British approach" to treating addiction. It was actually tried in the United States at the beginning of this century; in some ways,

the methadone maintenance centers — which offer methadone as a heroin substitute — now operating around the country are a modern adaptation of it. But back in 1912 and 1913,
narcotics-dispensing clinics were established in Florida and
Tennessee to treat drug addicts, and after the federal government restricted the distribution of opiates to medical use
in 1914, some 44 morphine and heroin clinics opened up
throughout the country. Federal authorities later closed these
clinics, contending, as did the British government in the
1950s, that they created a black market in drugs by over-
supplying the addicts, who sold what they did not use. Nevertheless, from 1919 to 1923 a clinic in Shreveport, Louisiana,
tried to treat morphine addicts by supplying them with drugs,
and for many years a small number of doctors in Kentucky
continued prescribing narcotics — mostly morphine — to addicts even after federal law prohibited the practice.

In the Netherlands, the government debated whether to
legalize heroin and distribute it to known addicts but ultimately rejected the idea. The Dutch policy is quite different

*In 1974, a Dutch vendor draws attention to his hemp plants, which were
then legal. Although marijuana is no longer legal in the Netherlands,
penalties for possession of small amounts of the drug are mild.*

A 19th-century drawing of nitrous oxide, or laughing gas, being given to participants in a "laughing gas frolic." This inhalant was used recreationally long before it won acceptance as a legitimate anesthetic.

in regard to marijuana, however. Although the use of this hallucinogen is not legal in the Netherlands, possession of up to one and a half ounces of it for personal use is punished with only a mild penalty. The Dutch even allow marijuana to be available to teenagers at specific youth centers around the country, believing that this will keep them from being pressured by their friends into experimenting with harder drugs. Similarly, Denmark and Italy basically ignore the personal use of marijuana — although trafficking in it and other drugs remains a crime in these countries, as well as in virtually every other nation.

Coping with Inhalant Abuse

The British approach to the problem of inhalant abuse — sniffing solvents, gases, and glues — is much like its policy regarding drug addiction: It seeks to treat those who abuse the substances — primarily children and teenagers — as patients requiring medical care, and to punish those involved in the sale of these substances.

The inhaling of mind-altering substances goes back to the late 18th century, when nitrous oxide, commonly known as "laughing gas," and ether, an anesthetic, were inhaled for "recreation" 100 years before dentists and surgeons first used them as anesthetics. The first reported misuse of liquid glue as an intoxicant occured in the United States in the late 1950s.

The psychoactive agent in liquid glue is a solvent called toluene, which depresses the body's central nervous system, causing mood changes that resemble drunkenness, as well as hallucinations in some cases. Other chemicals that frequently figure in inhalant abuse include halogenated hydrocarbons, found in cleaning fluids, and propane and butane, both of which are also found in spray cans. By the early 1960s, laws against glue-sniffing were passed in California, Maryland, Colorado, and New York; in 1963, Great Britain reported several cases of glue-sniffing; and in 1969, Japan reported 161 teenage deaths from inhalant abuse.

Although the British government does not view inhalant abuse itself as a crime, penalties are imposed on those who are convicted of selling inhalants to youths. Teenagers who engage in criminal conduct while under the influences of inhalants also can be referred to law-enforcement authorities for prosecution or treatment. Under a 1985 British law, the Intoxicating Substances Supply Act, a maximum six-month jail sentence and/or a heavy fine ($\mathscr{L}$ 2,000) can be imposed on anyone who supplies or offers to supply substances likely to be inhaled by youths under 18 years of age in order to get high. And in Scotland, although inhalant abuse is not itself a crime, misuse of such substances is a basis on which to arrest youths and refer them to legal authorities for treatment. Educational campaigns designed to combat inhalant abuse have also been launched in Great Britain.

In Japan, on the other hand, all drug abuse, including that of inhalants, is strictly prohibited, and no special laws have been passed to deal with teenagers specifically, according to the Japanese embassy in Washington. A survey done by the U.S. State Department in 1979 found that Japanese law provides for a prison sentence of up to 10 years for the simple possession of prohibited substances other than marijuana — for which the maximum sentence for simple possession is 5 years in prison.

An American who had been held on drug charges in Peru is returned to the United States. In 1982, Peru and the U.S. signed a treaty that allows prisoners to complete their sentences in their own country.

CHAPTER 5

YOU'RE NOT IN KANSAS ANYMORE

Many Americans who visit other countries mistakenly believe that as citizens of the United States, they are immune from prosecution under foreign laws or will have the same legal rights and protections overseas that the U.S. Constitution provides here at home. That can be a costly — perhaps even tragic — error. As the U.S. State Department has observed, being arrested in a foreign country can "ruin your life, not just your vacation."

In 1986, more than 2,800 Americans were arrested in foreign countries, more than a third of them on charges of possessing, using, or trafficking in illegal drugs. The majority of these drug arrests were for the possession of less than one ounce of marijuana or cocaine, and often the result was a heavy fine or a prison sentence. Although some countries have more lenient drug laws than the U.S., most of them have laws that are even tougher than ours, and many of the legal protections we take for granted under the U.S. Constitution simply do not apply overseas. You can be held in a primitive jail for months before you are tried, and you might then be sentenced to years in prison without parole.

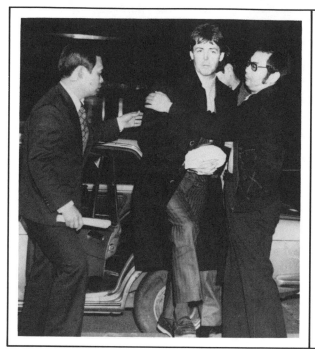

Singer Paul McCartney is arrested in Japan in 1980 for possession of marijuana. Although Japan normally imposes the maximum five-year sentence for marijuana possession, McCartney was jailed for only a week before agreeing to be deported.

According to the State Department, few foreign countries provide a trial by jury in drug cases; trials often are delayed or postponed for long periods of time, and when the trial finally is held, it will be conducted, of course, in the language of that country, which may be foreign to you. Sentences for possession of or trafficking in drugs can range from two to twenty-five years and may include a heavy fine; in a few countries, such as Australia, Egypt, Turkey, Thailand, and Malaysia, conviction could result in a life sentence or even the death penalty in some cases. (Six Americans are now serving life sentences in several countries for drug offenses.)

Americans were arrested on drug-related charges in 60 countries in 1986. Seventy-one percent of all the drug charges against Americans occured in five countries: Jamaica, Mexico, the Bahamas, the Federal Republic of Germany (West Germany), and the Dominican Republic. Tougher enforcement of local drug laws has also led to a growing number of Americans being arrested on drug charges in Bermuda.

Celebrities are no more immune to the strict application of foreign drug laws than are ordinary travelers. Stacy Keach, television's Mike Hammer, was imprisoned in England for six months in 1985 for trying to smuggle $3,840 worth of cocaine into the country by hiding it in a shaving cream dispenser. And in 1980, former Beatle Paul McCartney was arrested and jailed in Japan, which imposes a maximum five-year sentence for the possession of marijuana. McCartney, who was carrying a small amount of marijuana while on a musical tour, spent a week in jail before being released only after he agreed to be deported immediately. His concert series was cancelled at a considerable financial loss.

Midnight Express

Perhaps the most chilling and well-known case involving the narcotics-related arrest of an American overseas became the subject of a book and a movie, both called *Midnight Express*. They told the story of Billy Hayes, a college dropout who in

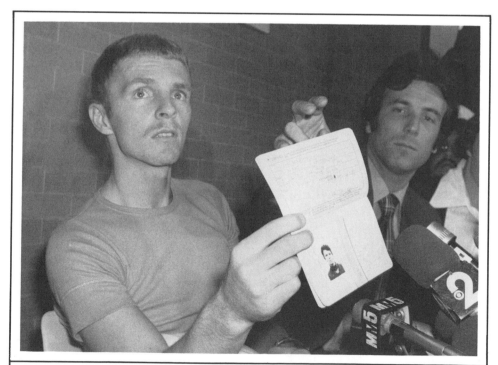

Billy Hayes, shown here displaying his U.S. passport, spent five years in a Turkish prison for hashish smuggling before escaping to Greece.

1970 tried to smuggle two kilograms (about four pounds) of hashish out of Turkey to take back to the United States. He taped the drug to his body, but it was detected by Turkish police as he was about to board a flight from Istanbul to New York. He was sentenced to 30 years in prison, where he was subjected to beatings and torture. He spent five years in Turkish jails before he managed to escape to Greece.

In 1979, the State Department conducted a survey of U.S. embassies around the world to find out what the drug laws were overseas and how persons arrested under them were treated. Although certain countries have adopted some relatively informal procedures for dealing with foreign visitors who are caught with small amounts of illegal drugs in their possession, the U.S. State Department warns that there is no legal, political, or moral code requiring other countries to treat American violators of national drug laws leniently. Another nation's police or court system may decide to prosecute or punish to the fullest extent of the law any American caught, for example, smoking a marijuana cigarette on the street — even if some "softer" treatment is available for simple possession of a drug. A defendant arrested for selling a single marijuana cigarette — or even giving one to someone else — could be prosecuted for dealing in dangerous drugs, or might simply be charged with contributing to "immoral" behavior.

According to the State Department, it is impossible to predict how the case may go for an American arrested on drug charges in a foreign country. "The wanton user, openly ignoring the dangers of using any illegal substance abroad, may be the American citizen who 'disappears' and is not heard from again by family or American officials for a very long time," the State Department says.

Catch-all Laws

Many nations do not have statutes that specifically outlaw substances other than marijuana, cocaine, or heroin and their derivatives, but simply include everything else — such as LSD, PCP, amphetamines, or barbiturates — under broad, catch-all laws against other "dangerous drugs" or "morally offensive substances." The range of penalties for possession of "other" illegal substances is as great as it is for marijuana, cocaine, or heroin. Eight countries — Austria, West Germany, Den-

Two Australians are led out of a Malaysian court in 1985 after being sentenced to death for drug smuggling.

mark, Italy, Nepal, Costa Rica, Paraguay, and Uruguay — allow possession of small amounts of these substances, but the definitions vary as to what a "small" amount may be, and it is possible that some substances may not be considered legal in any amount. For example, a country might permit people to have four doses of an amphetamine but jail them for a year if they have one dose of LSD. In fact, in those countries where any drugs considered "dangerous" or "immoral" are illegal, the penalties can be just as tough as they are for cocaine or heroin. The death penalty can be imposed in Burma, Indonesia, South Korea, and Malaysia for trafficking in "all other" drugs, as well as for dealing in marijuana, cocaine, or heroin. And 55 countries, including Belgium, Egypt, Greece, India, Norway, Spain, Switzerland, Chile, Costa Rica, and Ecuador, make no distinction in their laws between simple possession of an illegal drug and trafficking in it or cultivating it. In addition, 97 countries, including Austria, West Germany, Bermuda, Finland, France, Israel, India, Mexico, the Netherlands, Norway, Portugal, Spain, Sweden, Switzerland, Turkey, and the Union of Soviet Socialist Republics (USSR), technically have the same laws regarding all substances that are illegal. In addition, the application of the law in most countries is up to the individual prosecutors and judges. For example, a tourist in Morocco caught smoking a little hashish may be fined and deported — or may be sentenced to spend 10 years in jail.

Your American Passport is No Magic Charm

Many travelers who are arrested in foreign countries may sit in jail for a month or more before they are formally charged with a crime. Some countries do not issue a formal charge until the accused is taken to court for a hearing or a trial. If an American citizen is arrested in a foreign country, his or her chances of having the local police contact the U.S. consul — the State Department's representative in the area — are only one out of two, according to the State Department. In fact, many countries will not inform the U.S. consul unless the arrested person requests it — and often the police will not advise the arrested person of that privilege, or will not tell him or her about it in English. Sometimes the consul is not able to find out if an American is being held in jail because the country routinely refuses to give out such information.

Even if the American consulate is contacted, there are limits to what it can do. The consul can contact your family or friends on your behalf to get money for a lawyer or medicine if you need it; give you a list of local lawyers who are willing to defend you in court; and try to see that you are treated well and your rights under local laws are observed. But many countries deny bail in drug charges — even if the American consul requests it — and often the governments of those countries that allow bail are reluctant to grant it to foreigners because they fear that the accused person will simply flee the country before coming to trial. Many countries offer free legal assistance to foreigners who are arrested, but often the lawyers who are available are not the best. It is possible to hire a private attorney, but the fees are usually astronomical.

Although some countries have no penalties for the simple possession of small amounts of marijuana and its derivatives, selling marijuana is illegal almost everywhere, and is considered a serious crime that is dealt with harshly; sentences for this crime range from 10 years imprisonment to death, depending on the country.

Ten countries — West Germany, Italy, Austria, Denmark, Costa Rica, Paraguay, Uruguay, Bolivia, Peru, and Nepal — allow people to possess small amounts of coca leaf or cocaine. But 48 countries have laws imposing 1 to 5 years in prison for possessing cocaine; 27 nations impose 5 to 10 years for cocaine possession; and 16 countries impose 10 or more years on people convicted of possessing cocaine. All of the countries that responded to the State Department's survey impose at least one year in prison for trafficking in cocaine, and 75% of these nations (or 70 countries) impose sentences of more than 5 years in prison for this crime. Eleven countries impose sentences of 20 years to life for cocaine trafficking, and six nations — Turkey, Burma, Guinea, South Korea, Malaysia, and Iran — allow the death penalty to be imposed for cocaine trafficking.

West Germany, Austria, Denmark, Italy, Costa Rica, Paraguay, Uruguay, Nepal, and Bangladesh allow people to possess "small" or "minimal" amounts of the opium poppy and its derivatives, such as heroin, although the definition of what is a "small" amount again is not clear. Forty-six countries impose from one to 5 years in prison for heroin possession; 32 countries impose 5 to 10 years for this crime, and 14 nations provide for a sentence of 10 years or more for heroin possession. Almost 75% of the nations responding to the State Department's questions say that they have penalties of 5 years or more for selling heroin, and 9 countries — Turkey, Taiwan, Thailand, Burma, Indonesia, Guinea, South Korea, Malaysia, and Iran — can (and sometimes do) impose the death penalty on heroin dealers.

The Australian state of Queensland has that country's toughest anti-drug laws. Trafficking in heroin, cocaine, PCP, or LSD can bring a sentence of life in prison at hard labor. If the person to whom such drugs were sold was under 18 years of age at the time of the transaction, the life-at-hard-labor sentence is mandatory. A life sentence also can be imposed if a defendant is found guilty of having property that was obtained with the profits of drug-dealing. The drug sales could occur anywhere in the world, but if the property purchased with the proceeds is obtained in Queensland, the life-

Actor Stacy Keach testifies before the House Select Committee on Narcotics Abuse and Control in 1985. Keach had recently been released from an English prison, where he had spent six months for cocaine smuggling.

at-hard-labor sentence can be imposed. A sentence of 15 years at hard labor can be imposed for trafficking in other illegal drugs in Queensland. Other Australian states such as New South Wales, South Australia, and the Northern Territory also impose life sentences plus heavy fines for certain categories of drug trafficking, while states such as Victoria impose terms as tough as 25 years in prison and heavy fines for drug dealing. Although Australia generally does not have specific laws against inhalant abuse, the state of Western Australia, for example, prosecutes inhalant abuse under an old, slightly vague law against "any deleterious drug," which provides a maximum sentence of six months in prison for use of such substances.

The State Department advises Americans who need medicines that contain habit-forming or narcotic drugs to carry a doctor's certificate explaining their condition if they take such medications with them into a foreign country. In Saudi Arabia, the strict Islamic laws define as "narcotics" all alcohol, barbiturates, amphetamines, codeine, and many other substances that are not considered narcotics elsewhere. (For example, in 1987, a 26-year-old American businessman was arrested in Al Khobar, Saudi Arabia, for drinking alcohol and was given 60 lashes after spending a month in prison.)

Although Americans arrested in their own country have specific rights to counsel and a fair trial as provided in the U.S. Constitution, the situation can be quite different abroad. As a State Department official told the Associated Press in 1987, "Some people feel they can hold up their American passport as some sort of talisman and if they get in trouble, a consular officer will arrive and get them out of jail. It doesn't work that way."

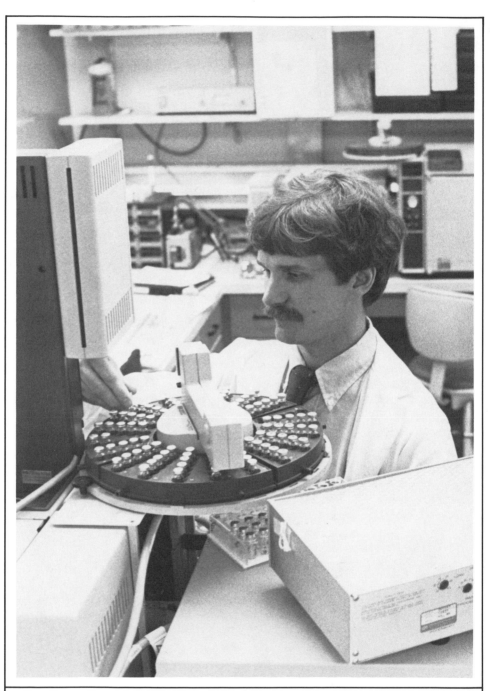

Dr. Barry Sample of Indiana University examines drug-testing devices. Drug testing is becoming increasingly widespread in the United States, even though many people believe it violates the right to privacy.

CHAPTER 6

DRUG SEARCHING AND TESTING

$\mathbf{D}$rug testing appears to be largely an American development. For years, police in most states have had the authority
to ask suspected drunken drivers to submit to a breath test
to determine if they have a blood-alcohol level that shows
they are intoxicated, but drivers can refuse to take the test
(although in some states that may result in an automatic
suspension of the driver's license). Urinalysis, or the testing
of urine to detect the presence of drugs in the body, is a
more recent practice, but it is a growing one and already has
produced a number of conflicting court opinions about its
constitutionality.

In the United States, urinalysis is being used increasingly
by employers to uncover the use of drugs in the workplace,
where employee drug abuse reportedly costs corporations
$33 billion a year. In 1985, a survey of major corporations
(the *Fortune* 500, the companies that magazine judges to be
the largest in the country) revealed that 18% of them conduct
some sort of drug testing on their employees. In 1986, the
National Institute on Drug Abuse estimated that 40% of those
companies were using urinalysis to test employees for drug
abuse. Hundreds of smaller companies have followed that
example.

You have to
scare the wits
out of
an addict.
Even if he sits in
the next office.

Nothing you do in business will
be much tougher than this.
    You may have to confront
your next-in-command,
the one you hoped would
someday fill your shoes.
    And you'll have to say,
"Get well or get out." There's
no other way for you to break
through an addict's defenses.
    But you're not alone.
1-800-843-4971 is the National
Institute on Drug Abuse
helpline for managers and
CEOs. Call Monday to Friday,
9:00 a.m. to 8:00 p.m.
Eastern Time. They'll refer
you to professionals who can
help your company set up
drug education, employee
assistance, and treatment
programs.
    Saving the career of the
guy next door isn't easy.
But who ever said being a
friend was easy?

A poster published by the Partnership for a Drug-Free America outlining how to deal with a co-worker who is an addict. During the 1980s the growing concern about substance abusers in the workplace has prompted many companies to institute employee drug-testing and other antidrug measures.

President Reagan ordered an extensive program of drug testing for federal employees in 1986. Workers in "sensitive positions" are required to submit to drug testing under procedures established by the chiefs of each agency. All other federal workers may be tested when "there is a suspicion that any employee uses illegal drugs."

Unreasonable Search and Seizure?

Although courts have ruled that the taking of urine specimens for drug testing purposes is a "search" or "seizure" as defined by the Fourth Amendment to the Constitution, it is not necessarily a violation of that section of the Bill of Rights, which prohibits only "unreasonable searches and seizures." Many of the drug-testing programs that have been established by employers have been challenged in court by workers who contend that the particular drug-testing program in question is unreasonable and violates their constitutional right to privacy. In Maryland, for example, a proposal to begin random urinalysis testing of state employees on a widespread basis was held unconstitutional. The Maryland attorney general said that urinalysis testing would be constitutional for those state workers whose jobs were not related to public safety only if the traditional "probable cause" justification for a search existed. Even employees in public safety jobs — such as state police officers and prison guards — were not subject to random testing, although a "somewhat more relaxed" constitutional standard — "reasonable suspicion" — would apply in these cases. "A war on drugs is a good idea, but not if its first casualty is the Bill of Rights," the Maryland attorney general said.

Other states and some major cities, however, already require the drug testing of some employees. New York, Pennsylvania, Delaware, Georgia, Texas, and California have drug-testing programs for workers on their payrolls, as do Boston, Washington, D.C., and other cities. The federal government now permits random drug testing of railroad safety inspectors, air traffic controllers, Coast Guard drug enforcement officers. A number of these employees have filed lawsuits protesting the drug-testing policy. The accuracy of specific urinalysis testing methods has been questioned in some of these court cases. The Supreme Court has not yet reviewed any of these issues, and the law on urinalysis testing remains unsettled.

Drugs in the Schools: Which Rights Prevail?

According to the U.S. Department of Education, the United States has the highest rate of teenage drug use in the industrialized world. Sixty-one percent of American high-school seniors have tried drugs. Forty-one percent of the seniors in 1985 said they have smoked marijuana, and 13% said they had used cocaine — twice the number who had used it in 1975.

More than half of the teenagers who used cocaine say they bought most of their drugs in school, and one-third of those who admitted using marijuana said they had smoked it at school. Two-thirds of the 1985 seniors who said they used amphetamines took them at school.

Surveys also show that the majority of students who use drugs get them from other students. This statistic has prompted government officials to consider passing legislation calling for regular drug searching and testing in American high schools. Since the Fourth Amendment to the U.S. Constitution — part of the Bill of Rights — protects Americans from unreasonable searches. In general, law-enforcement officials can search someone's home, person, or possessions only after obtaining a warrant from a court by demonstrating to the judge that there is "probable cause" to believe the suspect is doing something illegal. In the case of high-school students, however, the Supreme Court ruled in 1985 — and reaffirmed in 1986 — that school officials, unlike the police, do not need a search warrant or a showing of "probable cause" to conduct a search. They may do so whenever they have "reasonable grounds" to believe that such a search will uncover evidence that the student has violated either the law or school rules. For example, if a teacher thinks he or she has seen a student give a marijuana cigarette to another student, that is "reasonable grounds" for searching the students and their belongings to find the drug. On the other hand, such searches cannot be "excessively intrusive." For example, most courts have found that "strip searches" of students are not reasonable.

Federal law gives school officials broad authority to establish rules regarding student conduct. State and local laws also deal with the power school administrators have to regulate student activities, but those laws can vary from state to state and from county to county. In general, however, school officials can establish a wide variety of rules and procedures designed to prevent drug use in a school, although students do retain some basic legal rights.

For example, school officials can clearly state, in writing, what areas of the school will be subject to unannounced spot searches during the year because these are places where illegal drugs are likely to be used or found, such as student lockers, desks, smoking areas, or bathrooms. In most cases, courts have approved the search of lockers when school officials have given students written warning in advance that this may be done whenever the school wishes. Judges also have ruled in most cases that school officials or police can use trained dogs to sniff out and find drugs in desks or lockers, but courts in different states have disagreed about whether it is permissible to use trained dogs to "sniff search" students themselves.

Courts have ruled that if a student voluntarily agrees to it, a search is allowed even if school officials have no "reasonable grounds" for conducting one. But if students give consent to be searched out of fear — or because they do not realize they can refuse to be searched — then such a search is not legally valid. On the other hand, a search may be conducted even if a student refuses to agree to it, provided the school officials have "reasonable grounds" to suspect the student has illegal drugs.

Only a few judges have been asked to rule on whether high schools have the right to use urinalysis or other physical tests to find out if students have been using drugs, but so far courts have decided that urinalysis is an unreasonable search and violates the constitutional rights of students. In 1986, the American Council on Education (ACE) advised colleges and universities that if they wanted to test student athletes

Students in a California high school between classes. The United States has the highest rate of teenage drug use in the industrialized world; more than 61% of high school seniors have tried drugs.

A pipe used to smoke crack. The use of this highly addictive and crude form of cocaine has reached epidemic proportions in the 1980s, particularly among young people.

for drugs, they had to establish clear written guidelines for doing so. Such tests should be aimed only at detecting drug use that might affect the student's athletic performance, not just drug use in general, the ACE advised. In addition, high-school athletes who are being recruited by a college or university that has a drug-testing program for its athletes should be told about it well in advance, the ACE said.

High schools have the right to suspend or expel students caught using or possessing illegal drugs. Courts generally have ruled that whatever disciplinary action is taken against a student need only be reasonably related to the seriousness of the student's offense. In addition, if police charge a student with violating the law on the basis of evidence uncovered by school officials, the school does not have to postpone taking disciplinary action against the student until the case is tried in court. The school can also impose whatever disciplinary action it wants regardless of what the court decides. It is possible for a student to be found "guilty" by the school before the case is tried in court, and that student can be punished by the school for breaking school rules even if a judge or a jury has found him or her innocent of breaking the law.

State and local laws usually establish the penalties schools may impose on students for drug-related offenses. According to federal and state laws, students who face possible suspension or expulsion from school are entitled to be given advance warning of the disciplinary procedure and a chance to respond to any charges. The Supreme Court has ruled that a formal "hearing" is not required every time a school decides to discipline a student. For example, if a school decides to discipline a student for 10 days or less, it must tell the student of the charges against him or her and give the student a chance to deny the accusations. However, if the student's continued presence in the school threatens other students, teachers, or property, the school can remove the student immediately and hold a "hearing" later, according to the Supreme Court. More formal procedures are required if a student faces a suspension that will last longer than 10 days, or if permanent expulsion from school is a possibility. Many states have laws that spell out what procedures must be followed if a student faces a long suspension or expulsion from school. The flexibility a particular school has in such cases depends on the procedures detailed in the local laws. In general, however, federal courts have ruled that the student should receive written notice of the charges against him or her, a list of the witnesses against him or her and a description of what they will say, and an opportunity to present a defense and witnesses to counter the charges.

The Long Arm and Possible Consequences of the Law

If a student is expelled from school, state and local laws determine what effect that will have on the student's immediate chances for more education. Some states require alternative schooling for students who are under a specific age when they get thrown out of school. Other states say that an expulsion means the end of that student's schooling for the rest of the academic year. Some states permanently deny public education to any student who has been expelled.

School officials who seek to stamp out drug abuse in their schools may find that they have to report drug-related crimes to the police or help them uncover and prosecute drug offenders. A federal law, the Family Educational Rights and Privacy Act (FERPA), prevents the disclosure of information on a student's school record to anyone other than the parents, students, and other school officials without the written consent of the parents or students. However, FERPA allows the release of such information to police if they obtain a court order or a subpoena, which is a court's or prosecutor's mandatory demand for evidence. In addition, a health or safety emergency would permit the release of information on a student's school record under the federal law. The federal law also allows school officials to disclose the information on a student's record if that state has a law that was passed before November 1974, when FERPA was passed, requiring the release of such information to state and local officials. (Some state laws, however, may even further restrict the conditions under which a student's school records may be released.)

The federal law deals only with the disclosure of information on a student's school record. It does not prevent teachers or other school officials from telling police about something they have witnessed personally. If a teacher sees a drug transaction take place, he or she can report it to the police. In addition, drugs or other drug-related evidence that is taken from a student during a search may be given to the police.

A suspension or expulsion from high school because of an involvement with drugs does not necessarily mean the end of the world for a student, but it can have long-term after-effects that may limit opportunities for a college education and jobs later on.

Colleges and universities throughout the country have no uniform policy regarding the acceptance or rejection of students who have been suspended, expelled, or arrested because of drugs. Few if any admissions applications contain questions regarding drug use, and it is unlikely that a college or university would find out about a student's drug history unless mention of it was specifically made on the student's high school records. If a student's high school record does reveal a previous involvement with drugs, however, it could jeopardize that student's chances for admission to a college or university. Most colleges and universities have their own rules and regulations regarding student conduct, and some of them may deny admission to an applicant who has used drugs in the past, depending on the circumstances of that prior drug use and how it was uncovered and dealt with. The use of hard drugs may be especially damaging to a student's chances of being accepted at a college or university, because admissions personnel may fear that it is likely such drug abuse would continue in college.

Assuming a student gets into a college or a university, an involvement with drugs in high school can haunt efforts to get a job to help pay the college tuition, to enter a professional school, such as law school or medical school, and can even prevent employment in those or other professions. For

High school athletes during basketball practice. Although many adolescents experiment with drugs, others realize that this practice jeopardizes academic, athletic, and social performance.

Students stroll to their classes at Tufts University, a school known for its high academic standards. Although there is no nationwide policy regarding the admission of students with a drug use record, many colleges are reluctant to admit such students.

example, a standard application form for permission to practice law may ask the applicant to disclose if he or she has ever been dropped, suspended, placed on probation, or expelled from any school or university, and if so, why. Such applications also may ask for a complete record of all criminal proceedings — including traffic violations other than occasional parking tickets — in which the applicant has been involved, unless the record of them has been expunged, or wiped clean, by a formal legal proceeding. Applications to obtain permission to practice medicine may ask similar questions, and many professions, such as those involving engineering or scientific work under contracts obtained from local, state, or federal agencies, are likely to ask about drug use as well.

Drug use can remain part of someone's personal history for the rest of his or her life, requiring that person to explain the circumstances surrounding it whenever questions regarding drug use are raised. In the competition for jobs, a person who has been arrested for or involved with drugs — even long ago — is likely to lose out to someone who does not have such a record.

A headline-making example of the potentially far-reaching consequences of drug use occured in 1987, when Judge Douglas Ginsburg was nominated for a position on the U.S. Supreme Court. Ginsburg admitted that he had experimented with marijuana once as a college student and a few times when he was a professor at Harvard Law School. Ginsburg's admission immediately caused an uproar in the Reagan administration, which had made the antidrug crusade a major campaign. More significantly, it forced Ginsburg to withdraw from contention for the Supreme Court seat only nine days after his nomination. Ginsburg's plight is an extreme example of a person paying for mistakes made long ago, but it serves as a reminder that the potential consequences of drug use can be more expensive and long-lasting than any drug or the high it produces.

In 1972, members of the National Commission on Marijuana and Drug Abuse Control recommended that personal possession and use of marijuana be made legal. They also stressed that such use should be discouraged.

CHAPTER 7

LEGALIZATION? PROBABLY NOT

Anumber of writers and scholars who have studied the phenomenal growth of narcotics abuse argue that the quickest, most direct way of combating illegal drug use in the United States is simply to legalize that use. They say that the high cost of many illegal drugs — which causes many drug addicts to commit crimes to support their habit — is due to the fact that narcotics are available only on the black market. At the very least, some experts argue, the private use of marijuana should be legalized. If such illicit substances as heroin were legalized and distributed under government control, they contend, the price of these drugs would fall rapidly (since there appears to be an abundant supply of drugs), organized crime would lose one of its biggest money-making operations, street crime would be reduced, and the number of heroin addicts who contract illnesses — including AIDS — from using unsterile needles in unsanitary surroundings would decline.

On the other hand, there is a significant body of both public and professional opinion that opposes liberalization of the drug laws. Although legalizing psychoactive substances such as heroin, cocaine, and marijuana might in fact lower their cost, reduction in price alone would probably increase

In 1986, a 13-year-old girl from Tustin, California, turned her parents in to the police after repeatedly quarreling with them over their drug use. Here the Tustin police chief holds a press conference to discuss the case and to exhibit some of the drug paraphernalia confiscated when police raided the girl's home.

significantly the number of people who would both use and sell these drugs. Additionally, when society and the law sanction the use of a drug that use tends to become customary. This is evident from the examples of alcohol and tobacco. Moreover, legalization would inevitably make drugs more accessible to people who now rarely come in touch with them, thus further increasing the likelihood that use would spread.

Despite the fact that neither national nor international efforts to curtail the cultivation and distribution of psychoactive drugs have been particularly successful, this is no reason, antilegalization proponents argue, to throw up our hands. To write off prohibition as useless because it is hard to enforce, they say, is to surrender to defeatism. It is akin to saying that it is much better to surrender to a hostile invading force than to resist because the enemy appears stronger.

It is important to bear in mind that currently illicit psychoactive drugs are banned not out of petty moralism or intolerance, but because they have adverse effects on the mind and body, are addictive, and are potentially deadly. The public consensus is that the prudent course, both for strategic reasons and for public welfare, is to stand firm. The addictive substances that are already available and legal — alcohol and tobacco — do quite enough damage as it is. There is no reason to add to the list.

APPENDIX

State Agencies
for the Prevention and Treatment
of Drug Abuse

ALABAMA
Department of Mental Health
Division of Mental Illness and
  Substance Abuse Community
  Programs
200 Interstate Park Drive
P.O. Box 3710
Montgomery, AL 36193
(205) 271-9253

ALASKA
Department of Health and Social
  Services
Office of Alcoholism and Drug
  Abuse
Pouch H-05-F
Juneau, AK 99811
(907) 586-6201

ARIZONA
Department of Health Services
Division of Behavioral Health
  Services
Bureau of Community Services
Alcohol Abuse and Alcoholism
  Section
2500 East Van Buren
Phoenix, AZ 85008
(602) 255-1238

Department of Health Services
Division of Behavioral Health
  Services
Bureau of Community Services
Drug Abuse Section
2500 East Van Buren
Phoenix, AZ 85008
(602) 255-1240

ARKANSAS
Department of Human Services
Office of Alcohol and Drug Abuse
  Prevention
1515 West 7th Avenue
Suite 310
Little Rock, AR 72202
(501) 371-2603

CALIFORNIA
Department of Alcohol and Drug
  Abuse
111 Capitol Mall
Sacramento, CA 95814
(916) 445-1940

COLORADO
Department of Health
Alcohol and Drug Abuse Division
4210 East 11th Avenue
Denver, CO 80220
(303) 320-6137

CONNECTICUT
Alcohol and Drug Abuse
  Commission
999 Asylum Avenue
3rd Floor
Hartford, CT 06105
(203) 566-4145

DELAWARE
Division of Mental Health
Bureau of Alcoholism and Drug
  Abuse
1901 North Dupont Highway
Newcastle, DE 19720
(302) 421-6101

DISTRICT OF COLUMBIA
Department of Human Services
Office of Health Planning and
  Development
601 Indiana Avenue, NW
Suite 500
Washington, D.C. 20004
(202) 724-5641

FLORIDA
Department of Health and
  Rehabilitative Services
Alcoholic Rehabilitation Program
1317 Winewood Boulevard
Room 187A
Tallahassee, FL 32301
(904) 488-0396

Department of Health and
  Rehabilitative Services
Drug Abuse Program
1317 Winewood Boulevard
Building 6, Room 155
Tallahassee, FL 32301
(904) 488-0900

GEORGIA
Department of Human Resources
Division of Mental Health and
  Mental Retardation
Alcohol and Drug Section
618 Ponce De Leon Avenue, NE
Atlanta, GA 30365-2101
(404) 894-4785

HAWAII
Department of Health
Mental Health Division
Alcohol and Drug Abuse Branch
1250 Punch Bowl Street
P.O. Box 3378
Honolulu, HI 96801
(808) 548-4280

IDAHO
Department of Health and Welfare
Bureau of Preventive Medicine
Substance Abuse Section
450 West State
Boise, ID 83720
(208) 334-4368

ILLINOIS
Department of Mental Health and
  Developmental Disabilities
Division of Alcoholism
160 North La Salle Street
Room 1500
Chicago, IL 60601
(312) 793-2907

Illinois Dangerous Drugs
  Commission
300 North State Street
Suite 1500
Chicago, IL 60610
(312) 822-9860

INDIANA
Department of Mental Health
Division of Addiction Services
429 North Pennsylvania Street
Indianapolis, IN 46204
(317) 232-7816

IOWA
Department of Substance Abuse
505 5th Avenue
Insurance Exchange Building
Suite 202
Des Moines, IA 50319
(515) 281-3641

KANSAS
Department of Social Rehabilitation
Alcohol and Drug Abuse Services
2700 West 6th Street
Biddle Building
Topeka, KS 66606
(913) 296-3925

KENTUCKY
Cabinet for Human Resources
Department of Health Services
Substance Abuse Branch
275 East Main Street
Frankfort, KY 40601
(502) 564-2880

LOUISIANA
Department of Health and Human
  Resources
Office of Mental Health and
  Substance Abuse
655 North 5th Street
P.O. Box 4049
Baton Rouge, LA 70821
(504) 342-2565

MAINE
Department of Human Services
Office of Alcoholism and Drug
  Abuse Prevention
Bureau of Rehabilitation
32 Winthrop Street
Augusta, ME 04330
(207) 289-2781

MARYLAND
Alcoholism Control Administration
201 West Preston Street
Fourth Floor
Baltimore, MD 21201
(301) 383-2977

State Health Department
Drug Abuse Administration
201 West Preston Street
Baltimore, MD 21201
(301) 383-3312

MASSACHUSETTS
Department of Public Health
Division of Alcoholism
755 Boylston Street
Sixth Floor
Boston, MA 02116
(617) 727-1960

Department of Public Health
Division of Drug Rehabilitation
600 Washington Street
Boston, MA 02114
(617) 727-8617

MICHIGAN
Department of Public Health
Office of Substance Abuse Services
3500 North Logan Street
P.O. Box 30035
Lansing, MI 48909
(517) 373-8603

MINNESOTA
Department of Public Welfare
Chemical Dependency Program
  Division
Centennial Building
658 Cedar Street
4th Floor
Saint Paul, MN 55155
(612) 296-4614

MISSISSIPPI
Department of Mental Health
Division of Alcohol and Drug Abuse
1102 Robert E. Lee Building
Jackson, MS 39201
(601) 359-1297

MISSOURI
Department of Mental Health
Division of Alcoholism and Drug
  Abuse
2002 Missouri Boulevard
P.O. Box 687
Jefferson City, MO 65102
(314) 751-4942

MONTANA
Department of Institutions
Alcohol and Drug Abuse Division
1539 11th Avenue
Helena, MT 59620
(406) 449-2827

NEBRASKA
Department of Public Institutions
Division of Alcoholism and Drug
Abuse
801 West Van Dorn Street
P.O. Box 94728
Lincoln, NB 68509
(402) 471-2851, Ext. 415

NEVADA
Department of Human Resources
Bureau of Alcohol and Drug Abuse
505 East King Street
Carson City, NV 89710
(702) 885-4790

NEW HAMPSHIRE
Department of Health and Welfare
Office of Alcohol and Drug Abuse
    Prevention
Hazen Drive
Health and Welfare Building
Concord, NH 03301
(603) 271-4627

NEW JERSEY
Department of Health
Division of Alcoholism
129 East Hanover Street CN 362
Trenton, NJ 08625
(609) 292-8949

Department of Health
Division of Narcotic and Drug
    Abuse Control
129 East Hanover Street CN 362
Trenton, NJ 08625
(609) 292-8949

NEW MEXICO
Health and Environment Department
Behavioral Services Division
Substance Abuse Bureau
725 Saint Michaels Drive
P.O. Box 968
Santa Fe, NM 87503
(505) 984-0020, Ext. 304

NEW YORK
Division of Alcoholism and Alcohol
    Abuse
194 Washington Avenue
Albany, NY 12210
(518) 474-5417

Division of Substance Abuse
    Services
Executive Park South
Box 8200
Albany, NY 12203
(518) 457-7629

NORTH CAROLINA
Department of Human Resources
Division of Mental Health, Mental
    Retardation and Substance Abuse
    Services
Alcohol and Drug Abuse Services
325 North Salisbury Street
Albemarle Building
Raleigh, NC 27611
(919) 733-4670

NORTH DAKOTA
Department of Human Services
Division of Alcoholism and Drug
    Abuse
State Capitol Building
Bismarck, ND 58505
(701) 224-2767

OHIO
Department of Health
Division of Alcoholism
246 North High Street
P.O. Box 118
Columbus, OH 43216
(614) 466-3543

Department of Mental Health
Bureau of Drug Abuse
65 South Front Street
Columbus, OH 43215
(614) 466-9023

OKLAHOMA
Department of Mental Health
Alcohol and Drug Programs
4545 North Lincoln Boulevard
Suite 100 East Terrace
P.O. Box 53277
Oklahoma City, OK 73152
(405) 521-0044

OREGON
Department of Human Resources
Mental Health Division
Office of Programs for Alcohol and
    Drug Problems
2575 Bittern Street, NE
Salem, OR 97310
(503) 378-2163

PENNSYLVANIA
Department of Health
Office of Drug and Alcohol
    Programs
Commonwealth and Forster Avenues
Health and Welfare Building
P.O. Box 90
Harrisburg, PA 17108
(717) 787-9857

RHODE ISLAND
Department of Mental Health,
    Mental Retardation and Hospitals
Division of Substance Abuse
Substance Abuse Administration
    Building
Cranston, RI 02920
(401) 464-2091

SOUTH CAROLINA
Commission on Alcohol and Drug
    Abuse
3700 Forest Drive
Columbia, SC 29204
(803) 758-2521

SOUTH DAKOTA
Department of Health
Division of Alcohol and Drug Abuse
523 East Capitol, Joe Foss Building
Pierre, SD 57501
(605) 773-4806

TENNESSEE
Department of Mental Health and
    Mental Retardation
Alcohol and Drug Abuse Services
505 Deaderick Street
James K. Polk Building,
    Fourth Floor
Nashville, TN 37219
(615) 741-1921

TEXAS
Commission on Alcoholism
809 Sam Houston State Office
    Building
Austin, TX 78701
(512) 475-2577
Department of Community Affairs
Drug Abuse Prevention Division
2015 South Interstate Highway 35
P.O. Box 13166
Austin, TX 78711
(512) 443-4100

UTAH
Department of Social Services
Division of Alcoholism and Drugs
150 West North Temple
Suite 350
P.O. Box 2500
Salt Lake City, UT 84110
(801) 533-6532

VERMONT
Agency of Human Services
Department of Social and
    Rehabilitation Services
Alcohol and Drug Abuse Division
103 South Main Street
Waterbury, VT 05676
(802) 241-2170

VIRGINIA
Department of Mental Health and
  Mental Retardation
Division of Substance Abuse
109 Governor Street
P.O. Box 1797
Richmond, VA 23214
(804) 786-5313

WASHINGTON
Department of Social and Health
  Service
Bureau of Alcohol and Substance
  Abuse
Office Building—44 W
Olympia, WA 98504
(206) 753-5866

WEST VIRGINIA
Department of Health
Office of Behavioral Health Services
Division on Alcoholism and Drug
  Abuse
1800 Washington Street East
Building 3 Room 451
Charleston, WV 25305
(304) 348-2276

WISCONSIN
Department of Health and Social
  Services
Division of Community Services
Bureau of Community Programs
Alcohol and Other Drug Abuse
  Program Office
1 West Wilson Street
P.O. Box 7851
Madison, WI 53707
(608) 266-2717

WYOMING
Alcohol and Drug Abuse Programs
Hathaway Building
Cheyenne, WY 82002
(307) 777-7115, Ext. 7118

GUAM
Mental Health & Substance Abuse
  Agency
P.O. Box 20999
Guam 96921

PUERTO RICO
Department of Addiction Control
  Services
Alcohol Abuse Programs
P.O. Box B-Y Rio Piedras Station
Rio Piedras, PR 00928
(809) 763-5014

Department of Addiction Control
  Services
Drug Abuse Programs
P.O. Box B-Y Rio Piedras Station
Rio Piedras, PR 00928
(809) 764-8140

VIRGIN ISLANDS
Division of Mental Health,
  Alcoholism & Drug Dependency
  Services
P.O. Box 7329
Saint Thomas, Virgin Islands 00801
(809) 774-7265

AMERICAN SAMOA
LBJ Tropical Medical Center
Department of Mental Health Clinic
Pago Pago, American Samoa 96799

TRUST TERRITORIES
Director of Health Services
Office of the High Commissioner
Saipan, Trust Territories 96950

Further Reading

Asbury, Herbert. *The Great Illusion: An Informal History of Prohibition*. New York: Doubleday, 1950.

Bakalaar, James B., and Lester Grinspoon. *Drug Control in a Free Society*. Cambridge, England: Cambridge University Press, 1984.

Brecher, Edward M., and the editors of *Consumer Reports*. *Licit and Illicit Drugs: The Consumers Union Report on Narcotics, Stimulants, Depressants, Inhalants, Hallucinogens, and Marijuana — Including Caffeine, Nicotine, and Alcohol*. Boston: Little, Brown, 1972.

Burnham, J. C. "New Perspectives on the Prohibition 'Experiment' of the 1920s." *Journal of Social History*. 2 (1968): 51–68.

Cashman, Sean D. *Prohibition: The Lie of the Land*. New York: Macmillan, 1981.

Dolan, Edward F., Jr. *International Drug Traffic*. New York: Franklin Watts, 1985.

Freemantle, Brian. *The Fix*. New York: Tor Books, 1986.

Hamony, Ronald. *Dealing with Drugs: Consequences of Government Control*. San Francisco: Lexington Books, 1987.

Moore, Mark, and Dean Gerstein, eds. *Alcohol and Public Policy: Beyond the Shadow of Prohibition*. Washington, D.C.: National Academy Press, 1981.

Musto, David. *The American Disease: Origins of Narcotic Control*. New Haven: Yale University Press, 1973.

National Commission on Marijuana and Drug Abuse. Second Report, and appendices. *Drug Use in America: Problem in Perspective*. Washington, D.C.: Government Printing Office, 1973.

U.S. Department of Education. *What Works: Schools Without Drugs*. Washington, D.C.: Government Printing Office, 1986.

U.S. Department of Health Services. *Smoking and Health: A National Status Report*. Washington, D.C.: Government Printing Office, 1986.

U.S. Department of State. *The Global Legal Framework For Narcotics and Prohibitive Substances*. Washington, D.C.: Government Printing Office, 1979.

Glossary

addiction a condition caused by repeated drug use, characterized by a compulsive urge to continue using a drug, a tendency to increase dosage, and physiological and/or psychological dependence

AIDS Acquired Immune Deficiency Syndrome; a weakening of the body's immune system caused by a virus (HIV); thought to be spread by blood or sexual contact

alcohol any series of hydroxl compounds that includes ethanol and/or methanol; the intoxicating agent in liquor

amphetamine a drug that stimulates the central nervous system; generally used as an energizer, antidepressant, or appetite suppressant

Anti-Drug Abuse Act of 1986 comprehensive federal antidrug law with tough penalties for illegal drug possession or trafficking

barbiturate a potentially addictive drug that causes depression of the central nervous system; generally used to reduce anxiety or to treat insomnia

blood-alcohol level the measurement of the amount of alcohol in the bloodstream by taking a sample of a person's blood or urine; used to determine if that person is impaired by alcohol consumption

coca plant a plant grown in South America; its leaves contain many psychoactive ingredients known as alkaloids, the main one of which is cocaine

cocaine the primary psychoactive ingredient in the coca plant and a behavioral stimulant

codeine an alkaloid found in raw opium that can be used as a pain reliever and cough remedy

Comprehensive Drug Abuse Prevention and Control Act of 1970 a federal law that combined features of 55 statutes and created the schedules under which illegal drugs are currently classified

crack a less expensive, highly addictive form of cocaine

detoxification the body's process for removing poisonous substances or rendering them harmless; the liver often performs this function

distillation a heating process used to purify or separate a fraction of a complex mixture or substance

dram shop laws state laws that hold the owners of places that sell alcoholic beverages responsible in part for damages if they knowingly sell to an intoxicated person

Eighteenth Amendment the constitutional amendment, effective in 1920 and repealed in 1933, that prohibited the manufacture, sale, or transportation of intoxicating liquors

glaucoma an eye disease that causes the eyeball to harden; some physicians believe marijuana has ingredients that can help treat it

Hague Convention of 1912 an international treaty by which 34 nations, including the United States, agreed to control and restrict the production and trade of opium and its derivatives to the amount needed for medical use

hallucinogen any drug that produces unrealistic sensory impressions; some hallucinogens include LSD, marijuana, mescaline, psilocybin, and PCP

Harrison Narcotics Act of 1914 the first federal law by which the United States sought to control the importation, manufacture, and sale of narcotics, requiring those who engaged in such activities to register with the government and pay a tax on their drug-related activity

hashish an extract that is prepared from the flowers, stalks, leaves, and resin of the hemp or marijuana plant and that is smoked or ingested for its euphoric effects

heroin a highly addictive narcotic obtained from morphine

inhalant any substance that forms a vapor under normal atmospheric conditions

laudanum a mixture of opium and alcohol

LSD lysergic acid diethylamide; a hallucinogen derived from the ergot fungus that grows on rye or from morning glory seeds

MADD Mothers Against Drunk Driving; a nationwide group, founded in 1980, that works to have legal drinking ages raised and drunk driving laws strengthened and enforced

maintenance a treatment for narcotics addiction that provides an addict with enough of a drug to prevent painful withdrawal symptoms

marijuana the crushed leaves, flowers, and branches of the hemp plant, containing the psychoactive ingredient tetrahydrocannabinol (THC)

methadone a synthetic narcotic used in treating heroin addiction

Misuse of Drugs Act a law passed in Great Britain in 1971 that established special requirements for producing, possessing, and supplying otherwise illegal drugs

morphine the chief active ingredient in opium; one of the most effective pain relievers but extremely addictive

narcotic originally referred to a group of drugs producing effects similar to those of morphine; often used to refer to any substance that sedates, has a depressive effect, and/or causes dependence

nicotine the chief active addictive ingredient in tobacco; can act as a stimulant, depressant, or tranquilizer

nitrous oxide an anesthetic (also known as "laughing gas") that was one of the first substances used as a recreational inhalant to alter a user's mood

opiate a compound derived from the milky juice of the poppy plant *Papaver somniferum*; includes opium, codeine, and heroin

opium the powdery dried juice of the unripened opium poppy

PCP Phencyclidine (commonly known as "angel dust"); a hallucinogen originally developed as an anesthetic

physical dependence adaptation of the body to the presence of a drug such that its absence produces symptoms of withdrawal

Prohibition the period between 1920 and 1933 when the manufacture, sale, and distribution of alcoholic beverages were illegal in the United States

psychological dependence a condition in which the drug user craves a drug to maintain a sense of well-being and feels discomfort when deprived of it

Pure Food and Drug Act of 1906 the first consumer protection law in the United States, the act required that medicines containing opiates and other drugs indicate this fact on the label; it later required a listing of the quantity of the drug in the medicine and compliance with a standard of purity for drugs

Schedules the classification of illegal drugs established by the Comprehensive Drug Abuse Prevention and Control Act of 1970

subpoena a court or prosecutor's order requiring that a person turn over information or materials that may become evidence in a legal case

temperance the modified, restrained use of alcoholic beverages, often leading to total abstinence from them

tolerance a decrease in susceptibility to the effects of a drug due to its continued administration, resulting in the user's need to increase the drug dosage in order to achieve the effects experienced previously

urinalysis a method of testing a person's urine to determine whether he or she has ingested drugs or alcohol

Volstead Act the federal law that gave the government power to enforce the Eighteenth Amendment

withdrawal the physiological and psychological effects of discontinued drug use

PICTURE CREDITS

American Cancer Society: p. 45; AP/Wide World Photos: pp. 36, 38, 46, 50, 68, 70, 80, 102; Courtesy of NW Ayer, Inc.: p. 90; The Bettmann Archive: pp. 20, 21, 26, 29, 40, 42, 43, 49, 52, 54, 55, 76; Laimute Druskis/ Taurus Photos: pp. 93, 97; Reuters/Bettmann Newsphotos: p. 83; UPI/ Bettmann Newsphotos: pp. 18, 22, 30, 33, 35, 37, 56, 59, 63, 64, 66, 71, 72, 75, 78, 81, 86, 88, 94, 100; Richard Wood/Taurus Photos: p. 98

Index

Neil A. Grauer is a free-lance feature writer and former newspaper reporter who spent 10 years covering legal affairs, business, politics, and features. He is the author and illustrator of *Wits and Sages*, a book of profiles and caricatures of leading syndicated columnists. He is also the public affairs officer in the Consumer Protection Division of the Maryland Attorney General's Office.

Barry L. Jacobs, Ph.D., is currently a professor in the program of neuroscience at Princeton University. Professor Jacobs is author of *Serotonin Neurotransmission and Behavior* and *Hallucinogens: Neurochemical, Behavioral and Clinical Perspectives.* He has written many journal articles in the field of neuroscience and contributed numerous chapters to books on behavior and brain science. He has been a member of several panels of the National Institute of Mental Health.

Joann Ellison Rodgers, M.S. (Columbia), became Deputy Director of Public Affairs and Director of Media Relations for the Johns Hopkins Medical Institutions in Baltimore, Maryland, in 1984 after 18 years as an award-winning science journalist and widely read columnist for the Hearst newspapers.

Solomon H. Snyder, M.D., is Distinguished Service Professor of Neuroscience, Pharmacology and Psychiatry at The Johns Hopkins University School of Medicine. He has served as president of the Society for Neuroscience and in 1978 received the Albert Lasker Award in Medical Research. He has authored *Uses of Marijuana, Madness and the Brain, The Troubled Mind, Biological Aspects of Mental Disorder,* and edited *Perspective in Neuropharmacology: A Tribute to Julius Axelrod.* Professor Snyder was a research associate with Dr. Axelrod at the National Institutes of Health.